THE PSYCHOLOGICAL AND ETHICAL ASPECTS
OF MORMON GROUP LIFE

The Psychological and Ethical
Aspects of Mormon
Group Life

By

EPHRAIM EDWARD ERICKSEN
Professor of Philosophy, University of Utah

THE RELIGIOUS THOUGHT
OF E. E. ERICKSEN

Introductory Essay By
STERLING M. McMURRIN

A BONNEVILLE BOOKS REPRINT EDITION
THE UNIVERSITY OF UTAH PRESS
SALT LAKE CITY

ABOUT THE AUTHOR

Ephraim Edward Ericksen was born in Logan, Utah, on January 2, 1882. He received the baccalaureate degree from Brigham Young College at Logan in 1908, and married Edna Clark of Auburn, Wyoming, in 1910. In 1922 the University of Chicago awarded him the Ph.D. degree in Philosophy and Political Economy. In 1915 Dr. Ericksen joined the faculty of the University of Utah. He was Chairman of the Department of Philosophy from 1918 until 1948, and from 1942 until his retirement in 1948 he was Dean of the College of Arts and Sciences. From 1948 to 1953 Dr. Ericksen was Professor and Chairman of Philosophy at the University of Nevada. He was President of the American Philosophical Society, Pacific Division, in 1942. Dr. Ericksen died in Salt Lake City in 1967.

———

Sterling M. McMurrin was appointed Professor of Philosophy in the University of Utah in 1948. He was made E. E. Ericksen Distinguished Professor of Philosophy in 1965. He is now E. E. Ericksen Distinguished Professor, Professor of History, Professor of the Philosophy of Education, and Dean of the Graduate School.

THE RELIGIOUS THOUGHT OF E. E. ERICKSEN

STERLING M. McMURRIN

Professor Ericksen's religious thought and attitudes are grounded in the Puritanism that is built into the structure of American moral and religious culture. His puritan roots are found first in the Mormonism of his childhood and youth, which never ceased to be the primary determining factor in his life, and second in the pragmatism of his philosophical studies. Of course the Puritanism that persisted in Mormonism and pragmatism is not the Puritan theology with its absolutistic theism, original sin, and orthodox dogma of salvation. Mormonism, while exhibiting the forms of orthodoxy, is heretical in those very doctrines which were fundamental to Calvinism. Mormonism is finitistic in its theology and for the most part Pelagian in its conception of man and salvation. It is in its sociomoral character and its profound emphasis on the moral sovereignty of God that Mormonism exhibits its puritan origins. American pragmatism, on the other hand, though not in principle antitheistic, has had strong humanistic inclinations, and in John Dewey that humanism was consummated in a thoroughgoing naturalism. The Puritanism of pragmatism, like that of Mormonism, is found in its intense moralism and its social preoccupation.

Ericksen had a marked naturalistic and humanistic bent. He was strongly opposed to the traditional dualism of naturalism–supernaturalism and regarded it as a source of many of our worst social and moral ills. He was even committed to the defense and advocacy of a kind of cultural materialism. But for all this, theism appears to have been firmly entrenched in his sentiment and thought, although unconventional and unorthodox and often not expressed. He was not given to theological speculation and certainly his religious and theological views were not held or expressed dogmatically.

The Puritanism which Ericksen drew from both Mormonism and pragmatism was the Puritanism of the moral conscience and moral action, the deep-rooted consciousness of good and evil, right and wrong, a commitment to the Calvinist tenet of the sovereignty of the moral will, and the doctrine that the vocation proper to man is the creation of the kingdom of God. That in pragmatism this had become a secularized kingdom of man, the good society, made no essential difference to its sociopsychological drive or moral determination. Pragmatism, to be sure, has had many facets and it is not to be described simply as a moral philosophy. But the pragmatism with which Ericksen was intimate and which greatly affected his thought and disposition, indeed, the pragmatism that had much in common with the sociomoral character of Mormonism, the James–Dewey–Mead axis, was more than anything else informed by the last philosophical glow of the puritan conscience.

Dewey's philosophy has always been recognized as in some ways rooted in his New England puritan origins, and he himself remarked on the fact that Mormonism in action was a kind of practical representation of his own philosophy. In this connection Dewey exhibited some interest in the life and culture of Utah.[1] It was not, of course, simply the moralism but perhaps even more the intense practicalism of Mormonism that Dewey regarded with favor — but these are integral to one another.

Professor Ericksen's most productive period, from his Chicago years to the publication of his *Social Ethics* in 1937, roughly coincided with the best decades of Mormon Church intellectual activity.[2] He correctly regarded the Mormon intellectual era of which he was a part as essentially scholastic in character, devoted especially not to critical and creative activity but to the rational justification of the faith and the dogmas. But if it was a period lacking in the energy and robust adventurousness of Mormonism's earlier years, it was at least a time of considerable intellectual ferment, a time in which Mormonism made a marked attempt to be reasonable and to cultivate not only a rational theology but as well a rational ethics. In that quest

---

[1] Dewey's sense of kinship with Mormonism was reported to me by his longtime friend and colleague Professor William Pepperell Montague of Columbia University. In 1947 Montague told me that Dewey had on several occasions called his attention to the fact that some of the principles of his own pragmatic instrumentalism were clearly operative in Mormon social experience.

[2] *Social Ethics: An Introduction to Moral Problems* (Garden City, New York: Doubleday, Doran & Company, 1937).

for a reasonable ethics and a liberal approach to religion, Ericksen was the acknowledged leader. Whether in the university, at church, or at home with his family and friends, his was a vigorous and clarion call to reliable knowledge and reasonableness. He wanted to throw the light of knowledge and reason into all the dark corners of individual and social experience and thought.

Because of his apparent unorthodoxy, the Church was cautious in its approach to Ericksen, but it could not ignore his strong intellectual and leadership capabilities, and he labored intensively to join pragmatic philosophy and Mormon religion in a union that would satisfy rigorous intellectual and moral demands and both exhibit and strengthen those elements in Mormon thought and practice which he considered both valid and good. His primary interests were neither metaphysical nor theological; here he shared the pragmatists' suspicion of speculation. Rather, they were practical and moral. Ericksen was essentially a moral philosopher, and both his philosophy and his religion were incurably grounded in the moral conscience and moral experience. Here he was close to Kant, the chief modern forerunner of both pragmatism and liberal theology, as he was close to Dewey and to his own teachers, Mead and Tufts.

It is against this background of Ericksen's Puritanism and pragmatism and his interest in cultivating the pragmatic facets of Mormonism that both his social and religious thought must be described and interpreted. Indeed, his social, moral, and religious thought are all of one piece and cannot be segmented. Not that he believed that in some way Mormonism could be transformed into an institutionalized pragmatic or naturalistic philosophy. Actually, while intensely critical of what he considered the "priestly" conservative elements in Mormon ideology and practice and the authoritarian character of the Mormon Church — and indeed of most churches — and while impatient with the irrationalism, literalism, and superstition which he inevitably encountered in the Church, his attitude toward the fundamentalistic elements that were built into the foundations of both Mormon theology and popular Mormon belief was quite generous. His own religious views were unorthodox by accepted Mormon standards, even though they reflected the Mormon humanistic and materialistic inclinations, but they were basically theistic, with a strong biblical orientation that centered in a passionate commitment to the prophetic religion. In both thought and attitude he was a religious liberal in the best sense of that term, not seeking the destruction of faith, belief, or worship, but demanding that the Church and its religion come to terms with reason, science, and the dictate of the moral conscience. His was the first and last generation of authentic Mormon liberals, and he was their foremost philosophical spokesman.

Ericksen's doctoral work at the University of Chicago was well timed for producing a technically pragmatic impact on his thought. Dewey had already departed for Columbia, but his influence at Chicago was very much alive. George Herbert Mead and James Hayden Tufts were there, as was Edward Scribner Ames, and their influence upon Ericksen was strong. Here in pragmatism was the first authentic American school of philosophy, established by Dewey on technical foundations derived from Peirce and in the spirit of William James, a school of unconventional thinkers who were attempting to break new ground in creating a philosophical synthesis of evolutionary biology, psychology, and sociology with human values and political action. It was an attempt to construct a philosophy not in the traditional manner upon epistemology or speculative metaphysics, but on the ground of human valuation and social behavior. Ericksen's moral and religious thought reflect and continue this movement. His doctoral dissertation, published in 1922 as *The Psychological and Ethical Aspects of Mormon Group Life*, clearly exhibits in both its title and substance the determination to employ the instruments of empirical investigation in the analysis of values and to ground religion and ethics on the facts of human interest and behavior.

Somewhat like Dewey, Ericksen grounded his philosophy in what might be broadly called "social psychology." But his doctoral degree at the University of Chicago was in both philosophy and political economy, and he had a lifetime interest in economics. His concern for economic justice was joined with a passion for democracy, and both deeply affected his teaching. Here he was an advocate of what he thought of as a materialistic culture in which human personality could be cultivated and humane values achieved through the processes of rational thought and democratic political action. Always he opposed the abstraction of the individual from the social and natural context within which, he insisted, personality has its meaning and worth. In his presidential address of 1941 before the Pacific Division of the American Philosophical Association, "Materialism in Democracy — Democracy in Culture," he argued persuasively for the social ground of morality and defended the "theory of human personality that regards the self as socially constituted, so identified with the community that *himself* becomes merely a perspective of *ourselves.*" [3] It would be quite impossible to overstate the social context of Ericksen's treatment of the individual.

Professor Ericksen was committed to what he called the "genetic" method, the method of getting at meanings and values through the study of their origins and development. This was a common bond between him and the pragmatists with their large interest in organic evolution. In this connection he gave considerable attention to the development of morals in its relation to religion, especially as that relationship is seen historically in the Old Testament. Here he fastened upon the distinction between *prophetic* and *priestly* religion, religion of creative moral sentiment and action, and religion of conservative, authoritarian, and institutionalized legalism and ritualism. These large categories served him often in the discussion of both morals and religion and he applied them freely to modern and contemporary practice. His distinction between priest and prophet was sometimes more rigorous than his biblical models warranted, but it effectively served his purpose as a critic of established ecclesiastical conservatism and of religious profession that is devoid of moral works, and as an advocate of progressive change through creative moral insight and action.

The tie of morality to religion in Ericksen's philosophy was not based on any conviction that morality depends upon the sanctions of religion. His approach to morals was more humanistic, where the distinction between good and evil and the justification for the pursuit of the good are tied to human considerations — human judgment and the satisfaction of both personal and social human needs and interests. Nevertheless, he held that high moral idealism requires the "inspiration" of religion, where moral values are "motivated by reli-

---

[3] "Materialism in Democracy — Democracy in Culture," *The Philosophical Review* (March 1942), p. 139 ff.

gious impulse." "To ignore religion," he says in his *Social Ethics*, "is to neglect perhaps the most important single element of the ethical life" (p. 279).

On the other hand, for Ericksen, though religion is not essential to morality, morality is essential to the substance of religion. No religion can claim a high level of cultivation unless it has solid moral foundations. Indeed, at times Ericksen comes very close to an identification of religion with morals, insisting that "The religious spirit is the spirit of moral enthusiasm." He quotes with evident approval Matthew Arnold's statement that religion is *"morality touched by emotion"* (*Social Ethics*, p. 279). The identification is never complete, however, even though he does not define religion independently of moral values. Religion is "an instrument for moral conquest"; it is "a crusade, not a consolation," a faith in the capacity of natural man to create new values under new conditions. Here clearly is exhibited the prophetic facet of Ericksen's thought.

The pragmatic, sociopsychological treatment of religion that characterized Ericksen's philosophy is best seen in his *Psychological and Ethical Aspects*, which reports his impressive and discerning analysis of Mormon life. Religion is here not directly the subject; human behavior is the subject. But this is Ericksen's way of getting at the fact and meaning of religion. Mormonism's "essential characteristics," he says, "are not found in its theology. . . . To find the true meaning of Mormonism we must go to its group sentiments" (p. 8). The same is true for any other religious faith. Here, in the emphasis on the group, Ericksen clearly and fully exhibits the strong social orientation of pragmatic thought, especially as developed by Dewey and Mead, as well as the community and social character of Mormonism itself, in which he was immersed from his earliest childhood. Religion for him is a human matter and its meaning is to be found only through its function.

Consistent with his emphasis on the social base of individual personality, Professor Ericksen was not drawn to an extensive study of religion in its strictly individual manifestations. He was essentially a social philosopher and a student of social experience. Since in his view the individual person is incapable of abstraction from his social milieu, the individual's religion must be seen and understood in terms of the group experiences in which it is grounded. Accordingly, Ericksen treats mystical experience with some impatience. At least there is no indication in his writings that individual mystical experience should be taken as in any sense the foundation of religion. Religious experience described in such terms as Otto's "numinous" or "mysterium tremendum," for example, seems to play little or no part in his definition of religion. The meaning of religion is to be found in "spiritual values," but those values involve moral purpose and can and must be created, conserved, and promoted through human decision and action. They do not belong to some non-natural or other-worldly sphere.

The mystical experience is seen by him essentially as Schleiermacher's feeling of "absolute dependence," an emotional state that can be explained naturalistically and cannot be taken as the distinctive essence of religion. Of course it is not the naturalistic character of mysticism that for Ericksen disqualifies it as the ground of religion; he was in principle sympathetic with naturalism. Rather mysticism is something which cultivated religion should overcome because it involves a "yielding of the integrity of personality." Because it is irrational, it is of "questionable social worth." Here again the close tie of religion to morality is very clear. Indeed, religion becomes almost a handmaiden to ethics.

It appears that for Ericksen religion cannot be identified with any distinct or unique experience, mystical or even moral. Here he seems to be close to Dewey's position, set forth in *A Common Faith*, that religious experience is not a unique experience but is religious simply because it is taken in an experiential context that defines it as religious, i.e., an ideal context. This denies the full practical autonomy of religion, a denial which seems to be supported by Ericksen's statement that "Religion and Morality, considered as functions, are organically related in human experience" (*Social Ethics*, p. 279).

Yet Ericksen does not go all the way in Dewey's direction, a direction appropriate to thoroughgoing naturalism but perhaps inappropriate for one in whom there was a substantial element of theism and for whom God was not simply a theological idea or moral ideal but a living force. Though Ericksen showed little sympathy with whatever suggested the mystical experience — or any experience characterized by what he impatiently termed "emotional" — and though he opposed the traditional conception of the "supernatural," he held that men are in communion with God, indeed in league with him, when they engage creatively in the pursuit of higher human values.

In his formal definition of religion Ericksen did not neglect the "spiritual," though his conception of the spiritual as "purposive" was somewhat unconventional. He held that as "expressed on the inner side," religion is "faith in the spiritual or purposive control of life," while on the "outer, or social side," it is "active participation in the promotion of the highest human values." It is important to recognize, of course, that to define the "spiritual" as "purposive *control* of life" is for Ericksen to define it in somewhat moral and possibly even humanistic terms, as is also true for his definition of religion as a "way of living." [4] The crux of the issue is exhibited in the comment in *Social Ethics* immediately following the definition: "If it [religion] did not include in its scope both of these aims, it could not hope to add to the progress of the race" (p. 287). Here Ericksen's religion clearly exhibits his Mormon Puritanism with its Calvinistic and Judaic foundations. It exhibits as well the melioristic character of his own thought and disposition.

The characteristic optimism of liberal philosophy and liberal religion is found throughout Ericksen's writings, as it was a quality of his own personality. He had a firm confidence in the moral capacity of society to move steadily toward its ideal ends through reason, knowledge, and democratic action. The scientific spirit and scientific intelligence are already effecting a revision of religious ideals, universalizing them and making them more relevant to the moral life and the large interests of society. Of religion he says, "After long ages of oppressive ignorance and false ideas, courage and intelligence have largely triumphed" (*Social Ethics*, p. 284). This is strongly reminiscent of the optimism of the American Enlightenment and the

---

[4] Ericksen's definition summarizing "the essential elements of religion" is found in his chapter on "Religion and the Moral Life" in *Social Ethics*, p. 287: "*Religion is a way of living, expressed on the inner side as faith in the spiritual or purposive control of life, and on the outer, or social side, as active participation in the promotion of the highest of human values.*" His practical approach to religion, both his emphasis on faith rather than religious knowledge and his interest in the sociomoral facets of religion, is clearly exhibited in this definition.

nineteenth-century Social Gospel movement, from both of which Ericksen drew much inspiration.

Professor Ericksen's early faith in both the potential goodness of man and an ultimately felicitous outcome for the social order withstood the great shock given liberal religion by the two world wars and the intervening economic depression. Among the numerous works quoted in *Social Ethics*, written during the Depression, there is no reference, for instance, to Niebuhr's *Moral Man and Immoral Society*, Spengler's *Decline of the West*, Barth's *Epistle to the Romans*, Otto's *Idea of the Holy*, or any of the myriad writers who thought they had discovered the truth of original sin, a demonic factor in human history, or a new yet more sophisticated ground for the old religious orthodoxy. Ericksen refers, rather, almost entirely to the optimistic and melioristic social and moral thinkers who refused to abandon the old liberalism with its faith in human reason and human history, the liberalism that was expected to triumph through good will, democratic conscience and action, and the extension of scientific knowledge to the whole life of man.

The humanism, naturalism, and materialism that characterize Ericksen's thought must be seen within the context of a persistent theism that more often than not is concealed rather than explicit, a theism that is not less real or important in his philosophy because it is in the background rather than the foreground. Ericksen's humanism is the humanism of a positive accent on human nature and human capability that sees man as an instrument or co-worker of God rather than his enemy. He has no use for either the ancient or modern versions of original sin or salvation by grace. His naturalism is a revolt against the traditional supernaturalism in favor of a human alliance with nature; the highest values which man has achieved are the products of a value-producing nature. His materialism is not the antireligious materialism of the turn of the century. It is a materialism which insists that spirit and spiritual values are real but their reality is grounded in the material facts of human life, that religion is part and parcel of the psychological-social-economic-political process. Ericksen's materialism is more than anything else a denial of the distinction between the sacred and the secular, the opposition of the spiritual and the material. Here his Mormonism as well as his pragmatism is much in evidence.

Professor Ericksen's theism, which is not systematically developed in his writings, was of the Jamesean type — a conception of God that follows from a determined recognition of the facts of the moral life and a refusal to discount human experience as the ground on which to construct a theology. He had no use for a theodicy which sacrifices human freedom or the cruel reality of evil to the absoluteness of God. His was a finitistic theology, one which denies the absoluteness of God's power in order to justify his goodness in the presence of moral and natural evil, a finitism entirely consistent with Mormonism, whose basic heresy is the rejection of the traditional dogmas of divine absoluteness. Like James, to whom he was close in his personal religious attitudes, beliefs, and hopes, Ericksen approached theology with the agnostic caution characteristic of most philosophers, but with a natural piety and sympathy for religion that seemed to pervade his thought and persuasion. Like James also, Ericksen was an enemy of the absolute in all its forms. For him, the orthodox penchant for the absolute, whether in language, religion, morals, or knowledge, was the chief source of philosophical and practical corruption. To overthrow the absolute is to enter upon the road to a philosophy of religion that is relevant and meaningful in human experience.

Professor Ericksen was a big man — in physical stature, in interest, in character, ideas, and influence. He was the creator of a strong and enthusiastic philosophical tradition in his university, and his influence has reached far beyond the place of its origins. He was a teacher squarely in the Socratic tradition, determined to exhibit to his students the evils of irrationalism and dogmatism and to open their minds to the liberating strength of knowledge and reason, a teacher whose teachings and personality still inspire his students. He was a courageous critic of the social order, an enemy of authoritarianism in all its forms, a warm friend of youth, and a believer in humanity and the future.

THE PSYCHOLOGICAL AND ETHICAL ASPECTS
OF MORMON GROUP LIFE

TO MY
FATHER AND MOTHER

PREFACE

It is the purpose of this work to interpret the life-history of the Mormon group in the scientific spirit, and, in so far as the present methods of social and psychological investigation are adequate, to get at fundamental psychological and ethical principles. I realize, however, that the Mormon group life is extremely complex, as is every social unit, and cannot be stated in simple terms. I realize also my own limitations in dealing with the problem. One who has been associated all his life with the Mormon people, as I have been, is sure to have formed prejudices and conceptions which render an objective and impartial study of them extremely difficult. But on the other hand, the inner life of the group, its sentiments, and ideals, can be comprehended only by one who has actually experienced them. I therefore regard myself as justified in attempting to describe and interpret the sentiments which I have to a certain extent experienced in common with the group.

In this work I do not pretend to give a detailed account of Mormon history. The accounts of historical events have been purposely reduced to very brief statements in order to give greater prominence to the psychological aspects of the different situations in which the Mormon group was placed. It is the group sentiments with which we are here concerned, and particularly the genetic development of Mormon group consciousness.

In so far as I have succeeded in making this work scientific it has been through the influence of the instructors in the departments of philosophy and political economy in the University of Chicago. I am especially indebted to Professors James H. Tufts, George H. Mead, and Edward S. Ames, for the ethical and psychological point of view. For methods of investigation and organization of material I must acknowledge the help which I have received from the late Professor Robert Hoxie and from Professor James Laurence Laughlin, of the Department of Political Economy.

In the collecting of the material as well as its interpretation I am deeply indebted to my wife, who collected much valuable source material which I otherwise would not have received.

EPHRAIM EDWARD ERICKSEN

CONTENTS

PART III. MALADJUSTMENT BETWEEN NEW THOUGHT
AND OLD INSTITUTIONS

INTRODUCTION

CHAPTER I

INTRODUCTION

According to functional psychology, development in the life of the individual is marked by a series of crises. Meaning grows out of conscious behavior, but behavior becomes conscious only when a maladjustment exists between the individual and his environment. Consciousness becomes most alert and active when there is a need for adjustment. Under ordinary conditions instincts and habits direct the conduct of the individual but when a new situation presents itself these forms of control are inadequate and must be directed by consciousness. Instincts and habits tend to maintain that level of behavior already established, but it is the factor of consciousness which accounts for present standards of conduct; it is this extraordinary form of control which inhibits instincts, breaks up old habits, and initiates new modes of behavior. These crises may thus be regarded as the essential causes of the individual's mental attitude, his sentiments, and concepts, as well as the characteristic organization of his thinking.

This principle holds in social evolution as well as in individual adaptation. A problem presenting itself requires that the individual or the community change the old habits, customs, and thought and establish new modes of behavior suitable to the new situation. Any event, institution, or idea which facilitates or hinders this adjustment receives attention and is given significance. Thus historians are beginning to realize that the unity of history is best attained if the great problems which the people encounter are made the basis of discussion and if the historical events and characters are given importance according to the part they have played in the larger social adjustments.

This thesis is an attempt to apply the principles of functional psychology to Mormon history. The latter is here conceived as a process of mental and social adaptation. The discussion divides itself into three parts on the basis of three great maladjustments. The material selected for discussion and the points emphasized have all been determined by their relationship to these larger problems. The first part is a discussion of the conflict between the Mormons and Gentiles and is an analysis of the psychological and sociological factors involved. The second part deals with the maladjustment between the Mormon people and nature in

3

the desert region of the Great Basin.   An effort is here made to define the problem and to present the Mormons' method of co-operation employed in its solution.   We shall also observe here the reopening of the conflict between the Mormons and the Gentiles, caused in part by the economic competition between local institutions and eastern factories and business houses, which resulted from the extension of the Union Pacific Railroad into the Territory, and in part by the practice of polygamy which caused friction with the United States government.   The third part is a discussion of the present maladjustment, a conflict between the Mormon institutions and traditions on the one hand and the innovations of science and the new democratic spirit on the other.

In the present chapter it is intended to give a general description of the social ideal of Mormonism, its organization, and system of revenue. But, since the purpose of this thesis is to deal with ideals and institutions as they developed in the community, only those most characteristic need be described here.   There are, however, elements which seem to have functioned either positively or negatively throughout the entire life of Mormonism.   To state the factors in an introductory way may help the reader to see at the outset the nature of the problems.

Mormonism embraces the economic and the political as well as the religious life of its adherents.   Its ideals are temporal as well as spiritual. The material welfare of the community has occupied the attention of the ecclesiastical leaders quite as much as have the purely religious matters. Every president of the church from Joseph Smith, the founder of the religion, to Joseph F. Smith, the recent leader, has established colonies, built factories, and promoted mercantile institutions.[1]   The ideal social order is the "Kingdom of God" or "Zion," a concept which, to the Mormons, means a community of prosperous people as well as a community of righteous people.   To build temples in which the "pure in heart" might worship is a sacred task but no more so than to establish industries in which the "chosen people" might be employed.   The church is in reality a theocracy.   God is its supreme temporal and spiritual ruler.   Through his priesthood he directs the affairs of the commonwealth and of the religious body.   In this ideal order only one set of statutes or laws exists and they are God's commands which serve the purpose of both "Church and Kingdom."[2]

[1] "It has always been a cardinal teaching with the Latter-Day Saints," says the late President Joseph F. Smith, "that a religion which has not the power to save people temporarily and make them prosperous and happy here cannot be depended upon to save them spiritually, to exalt them in the life to come"—*Out West*, XXIII, 242.

[2] Keeler, *Lesser Priesthood*, p. 57.

But, according to original Mormon doctrine, the "Kingdom of God" cannot be built up under the present economic conditions. The individual accumulation of wealth must be abolished before the ideal spiritual relationship can exist. The highest spiritual and moral life cannot develop under a system of individual ownership. All wealth belongs to the Lord and it is to be used in the furtherance of his cause. Property and human effort have but one purpose, the establishment of Zion. The ideal economic relationship, emphasized more in early Mormon history than now, is called by them the "United Order." In the language of the late President Joseph F. Smith:

The "United Order" is a religo-social system communal in its character, designed to abolish poverty, monopoly, and kindred evils, and to bring about unity and equality in temporal and spiritual things. It requires the consecration to the church, by its members of all their properties, and the subsequent distribution to those members, by the church, of what were termed, stewardship. Each holder of a stewardship which might be some farm, workshop, store, or factory that this same person had consecrated—was expected to manage it thereafter in the interest of the whole community, all his gains revert to a common fund, from which he would derive a sufficient support for himself and those dependent upon him. The bishop being the temporal officer of the church, received the consecrations of these properties, and also assigned the stewardships; but he performed his duty under the direction of the First Presidency. . . . . .[1]

This order is regarded as a system patterned after that which the apostles of Christ set up in Jerusalem in which they had all things in common.[2] The Mormons also believe that it was this divine order which "sanctified the City of Enoch."

The term priesthood in the Mormon church stands for authority as well as signifying a special calling. There are only two priesthoods in the church but there are many degrees of authority. Each of the two orders or grand divisions is subdivided into groups of offices embodying different degrees of authority and demanding different kinds of responsibility. An individual, for example, is ordained to the Melchisedek Priesthood in the office of an Elder, Seventy, or High-Priest. Or he may be ordained to the Aaronic Priesthood in the office of Deacon, Teacher, or Priest. In general, offices in the Melchisedek order are higher and of a more spiritual character while those of the Aaronic priesthood are of a temporal nature and carry a lesser degree of authority. Such a distinction, however, holds only in a general way. Both priesthoods have, to a certain extent, both spiritual and temporal functions. All matters

[1] *Out West*, XXIII, 244.   [2] Acts 4:34–35.

of church interest are directed by officers in the Melchisedek priesthood. The president of the church who holds the higher order of authority has, in theory at least, unlimited power in all matters of church interest, both spiritual and temporal. The presiding bishop, who is also of the higher order, directs in all those matters which pertain to the collection of tithing and church revenues.[1] The local bishop, unless he, through revelation, is declared to be a direct descendant of Aaron, holds the Melchisedek priesthood. His special calling is to preside over a local church community and to direct in both temporal and spiritual affairs.

The revenue system of the church adds greatly to its strength and to the effectiveness of its efforts. There are three main sources of revenue, the tithing, income from property holdings, and free-will offerings. The first two represent permanent and increasing incomes, the third comes in the form of donations presented at times and in amounts determined by the need of the occasion and the ability and disposition of the giver. The tithing is like an income tax except that instead of having a variable rate dependent on the income, the tithing calls for 10 per cent regardless of what the individuals' earnings may be. The collection of tithing is, however, free from all coercion except such as the social and psychological consequences may impose. The following is the "commandment"[2] regarding tithing. It is typical of all the revelations which Joseph Smith presented to his people.

Verily thus sayeth the Lord, I require all their surplus property to be put into the hands of the bishop of my church of Zion. For the building of mine house and for the laying of the foundation of Zion and for the priesthood, and for the debts of the presidency of my church:

And this shall be the beginning of the tithing of my people; and after that those who have thus been tithed shall pay one tenth of all their interests annually; and this shall be a standing law unto them for ever, for my holy priesthood sayeth the Lord.[3]

The law of tithing was instituted in Missouri immediately after the discontinuance of the law of consecration or United Order.[4] It was not intended, however, to do away with the latter law. The United Order, although it is not often referred to by the present authorities of the church, is still regarded by many as the ideal economic system.

---

[1] Keeler, *op. cit.*, p. 116.

[2] The revelations of Joseph Smith are compiled in a book called *Doctrine and Covenants*. To the Mormon people its content is of great importance, ranking equal with that of the Bible.

[3] *Doctrine and Covenants*, Section 119 : 1–4.

[4] Joseph F. Smith, *Eighty-fifth Conference Report*, pp. 139–40.

The source of revenue next in importance to tithing is that derived from church property holdings. The church holds stock in some of the leading corporations of the state. Among these are sugar factories, salt manufactures, and mercantile institutions. It was the policy of the church, when there was insufficient private capital in the state, to invest in enterprises which it regarded as needful in the community. From these investments the church draws a revenue quite sufficient to pay the salaries of all church officials who are compensated by the church.

The free-will offering is much less in amount than either of the above-named sources. The bulk of these offerings is received on "Fast-day," the first Sunday in each month, which is a day of general fasting. The equivalent value of the food thus saved is turned over to the local bishop for the support of the poor. These contributions are immediately distributed to the poor for the purchase of food, clothing, etc. Another source of revenue is known as the "Relief Society" donations. Every woman in the church is expected to make regular contributions to this fund which also goes to the support of the poor in the church.

This brief analysis of the ideals and institutions which are most characteristic of Mormon life prepares the way for a more detailed study of the larger problems. These factors, combined with human prejudices and persecutions on the one hand and the forces of the physical environment on the other hand, have determined Mormon history as well as the present spirit and life of the group. The relationship of these factors and their relative importance will be made obvious when we consider them in connection with the great maladjustments of Mormon history.

But this attempt to define Mormonism in terms of its aims and institutions should serve only to give a general notion of the system. It is by no means intended to be a full description. The ideals and institutions have themselves only relative or functional meaning. Processes of elimination, modification, and accumulation are constantly taking place. Like every other social system Mormonism has been forced to adjust itself to varying circumstances. This has been true notwithstanding the tendency within the church to regard the system as universal and eternal and entirely beyond human control. And notwithstanding the appropriation of many of the ideals and institutions of ancient Israel the group has absorbed sentiments and ideas from its social environment.

This thesis endeavors to account for the structure and aims of Mormonism through a study of its life-history. The writer maintains that ideals were developed and institutions were formulated in the course of this history and that many of these ideals and the essential forms of social control as well were given birth through a strongly felt need for them. These institutions in turn reacted upon the life of the community, and thus the effect became also a cause. So important did these secondary causes become that many people have identified Mormonism with them. They have been regarded as its very essence. For example, to some people Mormonism means polygamy, to others it means communism, and others identify it with revelation, belief in divine authority, or conceptions of baptism for the living and the dead. Mormonism is not to be identified with any one of these doctrines or with the entire sum of them. Its essential characteristics are not found in its theology. A large part of its theology is copied from the Old and the New Testaments. To find the true meaning of Mormonism we must go to its group sentiments. If we are to comprehend its life we must analyze its spiritual life, we must study the problems which have confronted the people and the sentiments derived from the struggle with them. We must observe Mormonism in the periods of its greatest activity.

The great conflicts and struggles of the Mormon people, those events in the life of the group which have received the focus of attention and which were felt as vital experiences by the entire group, are here considered to be the essential causes of their sentiments and ideals as well as conditions out of which many of their institutions developed. We are thus concerned with analyzing problems, rather than following the sequence of historical events. We are more concerned with the attitudes, sentiments, and ideas in relation to events than we are with the events themselves. That which transpires externally is here considered less significant than the reaction which follows in the conscious life of the community. It is the ideals and sentiments resulting from experience rather than the experiences themselves which reveal the true life of a people. Special attention will therefore be given to direct statements and expressions of sentiment.

But sentiments are not to be regarded as independent of the active life of a community. They develop out of the social intercourse which takes place in connection with the larger economic, social, and religious problems of the community. The greater the problems are the stronger will the sentiments become. But these economic and social problems are to be regarded also as the effect of the psychological life. In other words an external situation becomes a problem only when it is conceived as such. The relation between the subjective and the objective life is reciprocal. The Mormon people were confronted by great problems in their relations with the people of Missouri and Illinois and in their struggle for life in the Rocky Mountain country and these problems created strong sentiments among the individuals who were co-operatively engaged in the struggle. On the other hand, these group sentiments thus created reacted upon the objective life.

To explain the Mormon community life in terms of its whole life-process, its conflicts, its struggles, its crises, is the problem of this thesis. Although there were notions advocated by Joseph Smith which were antecedent to the conflict and which really occasioned it yet these were not important in themselves. Had it not been for the conflict which forced them upon the attention, they would perhaps not have survived. It is group conflict and struggles which have created and maintained the basic Mormon sentiments.

PART I. MALADJUSTMENT BETWEEN
MORMONS AND GENTILES

CHAPTER II

THE ORIGIN OF MORMONISM AND THE
BEGINNING OF CONFLICT

Since the social point of view is the one proposed in this study the method to be followed is pragmatic rather than analytic. The special emphasis will be upon the consequences of the Mormon institutions and methods rather than upon the origin. Institutions are made and ideals are formed in the process of adjustment. Neither the individual consciousness nor the social life will indulge in absolute luxuries. If an idea or an attitude or an institution is to long remain it must serve some purpose, at least it must function in adjustment. The very fact that a social system continues and grows gives evidence that it meets some human need although it may be the mere satisfaction of a very primitive and artificial desire. The aim here is, therefore, not to pass judgment upon the absolute rightness or wrongness of the Mormon system but rather to recognize its problems and to evaluate its elements by considering the part they play in the solution of these problems. "In the end," says James, "Christian mysticism had to come to our empiricist criterion: 'By their fruits ye shall know them'; not by their roots. . . . . The roots of man's virtue are inaccessible to us."[1] Furthermore, the validity of a religion should not be judged by the neurotic constitution of its author. He says: "In the natural sciences and industrial arts it never occurs to any one to try to refute opinion by showing up their author's neurotic constitution. . . . . It should not be otherwise with religious opinions. Their value can only be ascertained by the spiritual judgments directly passed upon them."[2]

Joseph Smith met with extraordinary success in establishing his ideals in the minds of his followers. In less than a year he succeeded in bringing hundreds to his way of thinking. Before his death thousands had joined the church. What is the explanation? To the orthodox Mormon it is simple. It was the voice of God speaking through his prophet. Christ had called them and they knew the voice of their shepherd. It was the spirit of God or the "still small voice" which brought conviction to their souls. To the opposing religious dogmatist the answer is likewise simple. To him Joseph Smith was an agent of

[1] James, *Varieties of Religious Experience*, pp. 17–18.   [2] *Loc. cit.*

Lucifer. The followers of Joseph Smith were deceived. Satan had tempted them and they fell into darkness. Neither answer satisfies the true scientist who knows man only, on the one hand, through his social and physical environment and, on the other hand, through the response he makes to this environment.

Mormonism had its beginning in an environment, physically and socially, of a most primitive character. Western New York, the place of its inception, was in 1830 little more than a wilderness. The boy prophet was limited very seriously in educational opportunities. For him and his associates the Bible was practically the only literature. Schools were conducted for only a few weeks during the winter. The church was the one means of social intercourse. But this sort of social intercourse was found in abundance. It was rich with spiritual suggestions and dominated the entire social consciousness. Religious revivals were frequently held and the minds of the people were very susceptible to mystical phenomena. The stories of the Bible seemed very real to them and they naturally embodied their ideals in Abraham, Jacob, Moses, and other Old Testament prophets who talked with God face to face.

But in addition to the mystical and highly spiritual environment which was undoubtedly favorable to the acceptance of the new revelations, there were, in the personality of Joseph Smith, elements characteristic of a religious genius. He was emotional, impulsive and spiritual-minded. He was uneducated, yet he possessed considerable native ability. Few men seem to have such keen insight into human nature. This ability is manifest in his dealings with his followers. He never imposed his views upon them directly. He assumed the position of a prophet and spoke in the name of the Lord. In a most tactful way he held himself separate from the things revealed. Yet he was by no means lost to the consciousness of his people. On the contrary he was the prophet through whom God revealed himself; he was the means whereby the Lord was to bring about a wonderful work. Every commandment must be revealed through him before it could become law to the community or the individual members.

Another method which he employed was to present the revelations as nearly as he could in Bible language. This gave to them a divine ring. It made his followers feel that they were living a life such as that of ancient Israel, that a prophet was in reality presenting to them God's message. To a people who idealized the past as did the Bible readers of the frontier in the first half of the nineteenth century, such language was truly divine. The language of the Bible was the language of God. This ability to imitate the sacred literature was thus a source of strength to the modern prophet.

But Joseph Smith not only imitated the language of the Bible but he appropriated all the institutions and ideals of ancient Israel. And here we find the cause of the beginning of the great Mormon and non-Mormon conflict. The ideals and institutions of that ancient people were out of harmony with Christian tenets. The latter had made the other world the ideal home and resting place for the faithful. Mormonism, in its attempt to introduce Israelitish ideals, was setting up a material kingdom, a Zion on earth. To the Christian world, it was materialism against mysticism, carnality against spirituality. In the Tenth Article of Faith, Joseph Smith, in speaking for the people, says: "We believe in the literal gathering of Israel and in the restoration of the Ten Tribes. That Zion will be built upon this (American) continent. . . . ." This Zion was more than a mere mental state or spiritual order such as the Christian world held up as its ideal. It was a real country which was given to the Saints of God, an eternal home for scattered Israel, a land which was sanctified and blessed for the select children of God. It was a city which the Mormons were to build and which was to stand over against all non-Mormon communities. Here is the revelation:

And I hold forth and deign to give unto you greater riches, even a land of promise, a land flowing with milk and honey, upon which there shall be no curse when the Lord cometh:

And I will give it unto you for the land of your inheritance, if you seek it with all your hearts:

And this shall be my covenant with you, ye shall have it for the land of your inheritance, and for the inheritance of your children forever, while the earth shall stand, and ye shall possess it again in eternity, no more to pass away.[1]

Thus the Mormons were called out of Babylon, the country of the Gentiles, to inhabit a promised land just as Israel was called out of Egypt. They were the people which God recognized and to whom he would grant special favors. Note the resemblance between the foregoing revelation to the Mormons and the following to Abraham and ancient Israel:

And the Lord said unto Abram, ... Lift up thine eyes, and look from the place where thou art, northward, and southward, and eastward, and westward:

For all the land which thou seest, to thee will I give it and to thy seed forever.

[1] *Doctrine and Covenants*, Section 38:18–20.

And I will make thy seed as the dust of the earth: so that if a man can number the dust of the earth, then shall thy seed also be numbered.[1]

This promise was repeated to Israel.

And I have also established by covenant with them, to give them the land of Canaan. . . . .

And I will bring you in unto the land, concerning which I did swear to give it to Abraham, to Isaac, and to Jacob; and I will give it you for an heritage.[2]

In contrast with the material kingdom of ancient Israel and early Mormonism, with their land "flowing with milk and honey," their flocks and herds, and numerous posterity, is the Christian blessedness of the spiritual life and the other world, "the kingdom of God within you"[3] or the kingdom "not of this world," or the "holy city, new Jerusalem" which was already prepared and should come down from God out of heaven.[4] The kingdom of God according to Christianity transcends life. It is in a sphere beyond the carnal nature of man. This is true whether it is conceived as a gift from God or an attainment through righteous living; whether it is regarded as an ideal social order or as a quality or power within the individual. The one attitude which seems to have been held in common by all Christians is that the carnal nature of man is opposed to the highest spiritual life. Sinfulness lies in bodily desires and worldly ambitions, righteousness in spiritual hope, and a longing for complete union with God.

But it was the patriarchal order of marriage and ideal of a numerous posterity even more than the material kingdom which set the Mormons in opposition to the Christian world. The following from the revelation on plural marriage suggests again the source from which Mormonism received its ideals and institutions:

Abraham received concubines and they bare him children, and it was accounted unto him for righteousness, because they were given unto him, and he abode in my law; as also Isaac, and Jacob, did none other things than that which they were commanded. David also received many wives and concubines, and also Solomon, and Moses. . . . .[5]

Although marriage was conceived by the Christians as a sacrament, virginity and celibacy were regarded as the highest and purest life. "The virginity of the holy mother of our Lord," says Bruce, gave to celibacy a virtuous beauty that it had never before possessed. Many of the Christians of Asia Minor began, even in the time of the apostles, to

---

[1] Gen. 13:14-16.   [3] Luke 17:21.

[2] Exod. 6:4, 8.   [4] Rev. 21:2.   [5] *Doctrine and Covenants*, Section 132:37.

look down upon marriage; and in some of the writings of the fathers we find glowing descriptions of the superior dignity and spiritual worth of celibacy.[1] Tolstoi regards marriage as the service of self, and from the Christian point of view, even a fall, a sin. This being the attitude of the Christian religion toward even the legitimate monogamous marriages it is obvious that a religion which advocated "many wives and concubines" would be condemned as sensual and directly opposed to Christ's spirit and true religion.

But the materialism in Mormonism is also in part accounted for by the fact that it originated at a time when there was considerable interest taken in communistic enterprises. It was between 1824 and 1830 that Robert Owen established his communistic societies in different parts of the country and especially in the West. Two such communities were established in Ohio, one at Kendal and the other at Yellow Springs. In fact, the nucleus of the first Mormon community was a small communistic society, living at Kirtland, Ohio. The members of this society, before conversion to the Mormon faith, were members of the Disciples of Christ. Practically the entire community joined the Mormon church.

It is also significant that among those who left the Disciples' church to join the Mormons was one of its preachers, Sidney Rigdon. In fact, according to H. H. Bancroft, it was out of the "friendship and association" between Alexander Campbell, Walter Scott, and Sidney Rigdon that the Disciples or Campbellites' church arose.[2] Rigdon undoubtedly became interested in Robert Owen's communistic system through the famous debates carried on between his friend, Campbell, and Owen in 1829[3] (one year before the Mormon church was organized). During the early years when the ideals and institutions of Mormonism were taking shape, Rigdon was intimately associated with Joseph Smith, standing in authority next to him for a number of years. It is very probable, therefore, that Rigdon carried over into Mormonism Owen's communistic doctrine so generally discussed at that time.

[1] W. S. Bruce, *Social Aspects of Christian Morality*, pp. 66–67.

[2] H. H. Bancroft, *History of Utah*, p. 76.

[3] John H. Noyes, *History of American Socialism*, p. 87.

CHAPTER III

ZION IN MISSOURI—GROUP CONSCIOUSNESS
AS THE CAUSE OF CONFLICT

It was in Jackson County, Missouri, that the prophet had hoped to fully realize his ideal social scheme. This was the "land of Promise" and "blessed above all other lands." Even today the Mormons refer to Jackson County as the "Center Stake of Zion" and look forward to the time when they may reinhabit this sacred place. Great care was taken in the selection of those who were to settle on the "Promised Land." Only the worthy were to have inheritance there; only those who had fully entered into the Mormon group spirit and were willing to consecrate all their property and be content with such an amount as the bishop thought was actually needed. Every man who would join the new community was required to present a certificate from the bishop at Kirtland as a proof that he was a "wise steward" and worthy of this special blessing.

In August, 1831, the first settlers were received by the authorities who had previously been appointed to buy the land and to "divide unto the Saints their inheritance." The laying of the first log for the building of the first house was an occasion of celebration and ceremony. It was placed by twelve men "in honor of the twelve tribes of Israel." The ceremony of the dedication of the land distributed among the favored pioneers is significant as showing the sacredness with which they regarded their Zion.

Sidney Rigdon stood before the Saints and asked: "Do you receive this land of your inheritance with thankful hearts, from the Lord?"

The audience responded: "We do."

"Do you pledge yourselves to keep the law of God on this land, which you never kept in your own land?"

"We do."

"Do you pledge yourselves to see that others of your brethren who shall come hither do keep the laws of God?"

"We do."

Prayer was then offered and the ceremony ended with the words: "I now promise this land, consecrated and dedicated unto the Lord for a possession and inheritance for the Saints and for all the faithful servants of the Lord, to the remotest ages of time, in the name of Jesus Christ having authority from him. Amen."[1]

---

[1] Evans, *Hundred Years of Mormonism*, pp. 144–50.

These ceremonies suggest the key of the entire struggle between the Mormons and Gentiles in Missouri. The causes of the persecutions are not explained by assuming, as many Mormons do, that the people of Missouri were possessed with bad motives or evil spirits. There probably were many immoral acts committed by individuals among both Mormons and Gentiles and there were undoubtedly many evil-spirited men, even human devils engaged in this warfare, but no more perhaps than could be found in any other frontier community in the country. The causes of the antagonism were psychological. There are unsocial tendencies in human nature which, under certain conditions, will express themselves regardless of the moral attainments of the people. All peoples are at times creatures of group consciousness and group morality as has been plainly illustrated in the recent world-war. The soldiers of one army did not hate the soldiers of the opposing army for anything that they had done as individuals but because they belonged to another group. The Gentiles did not despise the Mormons because of any acts of individuals but because they were Mormons and had set themselves over against all the old settlers of Missouri. Three causes were responsible for the group animosity; these were: (1) purely religious differences, (2) the claim which the Mormons made to land of their Zion, and (3) their attitude toward the negroes.

That the Mormon persecution in Jackson County arose essentially out of differences of religious belief is evident from the content of what was termed the "Secret Constitution," a document by which the non-Mormons of the county bound themselves together for the purpose of expelling the Mormons from the state. The document contains the following:

It is more than two years since the first of these fanatics, or knaves (for one or the other they undoubtedly are) made their appearance first amongst us, and pretended as they did, and now do, to hold personal communication and converse face to face with the most High God; to receive communications and revelations direct from heaven; to heal the sick by the laying on of hands; and, in short, to perform all the wonder working miracles wrought by the inspired Apostles and Prophets of old. . . . . They openly blaspheme the Most High God and cast contempt on his holy religion, by pretending to receive revelations direct from heaven, by pretending to speak unknown tongues, by direct inspiration and by diverse pretenses derogatory to God and religion and to utter subversion of human reason.[1]

[1] Joseph Smith, *History of the Church*, I, 378. The document was copied from the *Evening and Morning Star* of July, 1833.

Thus, it was not for crimes committed nor for immoral motives that the residents of Jackson County expelled the Mormons but for pretending to have heavenly communication and for possessing spiritual gifts. In other words the beliefs and extraordinary pretentions had made the Mormons a group different from their own. Group consciousness and group morality developed. The individual shifted his personal responsibility upon the group to which he belonged. He lost sight of his personal ideals and sacrificed himself entirely to the group. In this state of mind the individual was led to do things that he otherwise would not do.[1]

Again the Saints declared openly that God had given them the land which both Mormons and Missourians then occupied and even in revelation were they told that the "obedient shall eat the good of the land of Zion . . . . " and the rebellious "shall be plucked out."[2] Although no attempt had been made to gain possession of the land by any means other than by purchase it was rumored that if the land could not be bought some other method might be employed. But rumors were about as effective as knowledge in developing emotions of antagonism. The Mormons had already been made to regard themselves as God's favored ones. It was they who had been blessed with a prophet, with revelations, with spiritual gifts and with a land for their eternal inheritance. The Missourians, on the other hand, were conscious of belonging to a righteous band whose task it was to put an end to the Mormon blasphemy and protect their land from Mormon invasion. Both groups felt that they were fighting for Christ and pure religion.

This group prejudice was further intensified by the fact that the Mormons came from the northern and New England states while the old settlers of Jackson County came from the southern states. Consequently the two groups differed in attitude toward slavery. The Mormons were charged with sowing dissension and raising sedition among the slaves and inviting free people of color to settle in Jackson County. The Mormons denied these charges and declared in their official paper, the *Evening and Morning Star*,[3] that the church had taken no definite stand on the subject of slavery and that "wisdom would dictate great care among the branches of the church of Christ on this subject. So long as we have no special rules in the Church, as to people of color, let prudence guide, and while they as well as we, are in the hands of a merci-

[1] *Doctrine and Covenants*, Section 64: 27–30.
[2] *Ibid.*, 35–36.
[3] *Evening and Morning Star Extra*, July 16, 1833.

ful God, we say: shun every appearance of evil." This was interpreted to mean that negroes and mulattoes were being invited to become Mormons and settle in the county. Such misinterpretation illustrates how easy it is to find cause for complaint when there is really, as in this case, a long established prejudice. It was not this article nor any particular act of the Mormons or the Gentiles that caused the enmity. This was only an occasion for the expression of prejudices already existent.

A mere enumeration of acts of misbehavior on the part of either group will not explain the cause of the struggle. These events are only outward manifestations of forces more fundamental. The causes are more deeply rooted. The struggle was not one of individuals against individuals but rather one of group against group.

This spirit of enmity grew until the winter of 1833, when it expressed itself in open violences. The leaders of the church were tarred and feathered, property was destroyed, and the entire Mormon population, which had now reached twelve thousand, was driven into the wilderness. Most of the exiles moved north into Clay County. Having been obliged to leave most of their goods and chattels behind, they were poorly prepared to withstand the winter cold that was then upon them.

The people of Clay County, however, were kindly disposed toward the Mormons, permitting them to occupy vacant cabins, employing some of the men on the farms, some of the women as domestic servants, and others as school teachers. A few families were able to purchase homes but the majority either rented land or were hired to the citizens of the county. But the sympathetic attitude which the citizens of Clay County at first manifested toward the Mormons was short-lived. The Gentiles here had no more in common with the Mormons than did the Gentiles of Jackson County and it was not long before the inhabitants of Clay County learned to regard the Mormons as a distinct and peculiar people. In less than three years they began to take actions to rid themselves of their new neighbors. On June 29, 1836, the citizens assembled in the courthouse to consider possible means for inducing the Mormons to leave their country. It is interesting to observe that here, as in Jackson County, it was not overt acts or series of crimes which caused the citizens to feel uncomfortable in the presence of the Mormons but rather an indefinable something that made the Mormon group different from their own. An extract from the minutes of the citizens illustrates the situation:

They are Eastern men, whose manners, habits, customs, and even dialect, are essentially different from our own. They are non-slaveholders, and opposed to slavery, which in this peculiar period, when abolition has reared its deformed and haggard visage in our land, is well calculated to excite deep and abiding prejudices in any community where slavery is tolerated and protected.

In addition to all this, they are charged, as they have hitherto been, with keeping up a constant communication with our Indian tribes on our frontiers, with declaring, even from the pulpit, that the Indians are a part of God's chosen people and are destined by heaven to inherit this land, in common with themselves. We do not vouch for the correctness of these statements; but whether they are true or false, their effect has been the same in exciting our community.[1]

Thus the Saints were requested to leave Clay County, not because of misconduct either legally or morally, but because their religious tenets, their habits, customs, dialect, etc., were different from those of the other inhabitants. They were asked to leave because they were non-slaveholders and because they declared the Indians to be their brethren. What could more clearly express group psychology and even group morality than these accusations? Human society is so constituted that unless individuals of the different groups can find something in common they will not associate. The Mormons refused to have anything in common with their Gentile neighbors and consequently the only thing that would insure peace was isolation. This fact was now beginning to be recognized by both Mormons and Gentiles.

To avoid serious persecution such as they suffered in Jackson County the Saints moved at once into the territory attached to Ray County. They petitioned the state for the privilege of organizing into a county. Their petition was granted and the Mormons thus became the founders of Caldwell County. Here the Saints grew rapidly in wealth and population. By the autumn of 1838 they had opened in Caldwell and adjoining counties two thousand farms and had erected many houses, hotels, stores, and shops of all kinds.

The Saints were beginning to feel that they had now come to a realization of their hopes. God had in a sort of indirect way led them to a place where they were to enjoy peace and prosperity.[2] This seemed to give them a feeling of strength and courage and, in the case of some individuals, resulted in a boldness which had serious consequences. For example, Sidney Rigdon unwisely gave expression to his feelings in a Fourth of July speech in 1838. The following is an extract from his oration:

[1] Joseph Smith, *op. cit.*, I, 450.
[2] H. H. Bancroft, *Bancroft's Works*, XXVI, 119.

We take God to witness and the holy angels to witness this day that we warn all men, in the name of Jesus Christ, to come on us no more forever. The man or set of men who attempt it, do it at the expense of their lives; and that mob that comes on us to disturb us, there shall be between us and them a war of extermination, for we will follow them till the last drop of blood is spilled, or else they will have to exterminate us for we will carry the war to their own houses, and their own families, and one party or the other shall be utterly destroyed.[1]

But Rigdon's pride was soon humbled and the prosperity of the Saints was soon to be replaced by poverty. The two years of peace was but a calm before the storm. A disturbance in Davis County in August of that year marks the beginning of the trouble which finally resulted in the expulsion of the Mormons from the state. Attempts were made to prevent certain Mormons from voting. The latter insisted upon their rights as American citizens and cast their votes, but not until after a skirmish in which several on both sides were wounded. News of this circumstance spread like wildfire through Davis and Caldwell counties. A general uprising followed. The leading citizens tried to quiet matters but to no avail. Conditions went from bad to worse. Finally the affairs became so alarming that Major-General Atchison called out the militia of Ray and Clay counties under the command of Generals Doniphan and Parks. General Parks with a small army went to Davis County and Doniphan with a small body of men went to Dewit to put down a mob uprising at that place.

That the Saints must again leave their homes became evident. They all gathered at Far West, the county seat of Caldwell, and from there they were compelled in midwinter to leave the state. Generals Doniphan and Parks endeavored faithfully to protect the Mormons from mob-violence, but with little avail for they were struggling against too many odds. They were outnumbered by the mob and their own soldiers were, themselves, prejudiced against the Mormons. Governor Boggs remained indifferent at first and maintained that since the Mormons had brought the trouble upon themselves it was left with them to fight it out with the mob. He could give them no help. Later, however, for no good reason yet known to historians, he ordered General Clark to rally the state militia and drive the Mormons from the state.

Attention should be directed toward two significant results of the Mormon residence in Missouri. In the first place Mormon group consciousness was taking definite form. The rapid building up of a colony

[1] *Ibid.*, p. 120.

in a county, and quick development of prejudice and persecution convinced the Mormons as well as the non-Mormons that the two groups had nothing in common. Not knowing the cause of the bitter hatred between the groups and the sympathy which developed within the groups, a mysticism was apparent in the consciousness of both. God symbolized the spirit of love which the members of the same group bore toward one another, and the devil symbolized the spirit of hatred which existed between the groups.

In the second place the Mormon social ideal or Zion also received its definite form. Jackson County, Missouri, is to this day regarded by the Saints as sacred land on which they are to build their Zion. This concept has played no small part in Mormon history since the expulsion from Missouri and it is sure to play an important part in the future.

CHAPTER IV

ZION IN ILLINOIS—AN INDEPENDENT CITY

Driven from Missouri the Saints found refuge in Illinois. There our story repeats itself. From one community they were expelled by an armed force and in another received with open arms of friendship. In one state they were deprived of their homes and property; in another they were given shelter, food, and clothing. In one state they were considered outlaws and deprived of the rights of citizenship; in another state they were not only given the rights of citizenship but were permitted to establish an independent city whose charter allowed them to organize an army for protection. Why the attitude of these two friendly states should be so different toward the Mormons, historians have thus far failed to answer. It is obvious that, had the Mormons been expelled from Missouri on account of theft, murder, or any illegal or immoral conduct whatsoever, knowledge of this would have been had by the people east of the Mississippi and their reception would have been very different.

But the Mormons were expelled from Missouri not on account of criminality but because of peculiarity. They were expelled for reasons that could not be easily communicated. They were driven out because they practiced their creed, "mind your own business." They believed that their business was absolutely distinct from that of their gentile neighbors. They had their own peculiar religious interests, their own economic order, and to a certain extent their own political interest and control. They desired no interest or co-operative intercourse with people outside of their own group. Such an attitude will be treated with indifference for a short time, but an entire absence of common interests leads inevitably to a severance of friendly relations. This was repeatedly illustrated in Missouri and later in Illinois. Two peoples cannot live together unless there is some common ground, some natural interest or condition for co-operation. It is a vital principle in human society that "he who is not for us is against us." Human nature cannot tolerate indifference. Only by association could the people of Illinois be made to understand that the Mormon people were not to become one with them.

Quincy, Illinois, became the resting-place for the greater number of the Saints until a permanent place was determined upon. But the prophet was not long in selecting another Zion.   Commerce, Hancock County, was soon selected as the central spot for the new community. Though at that time swampy and unhealthful it was conveniently located as it was almost encircled by the Mississippi.   It was drained of its impure water, renamed, and became in a short time the beautiful city of Nauvoo.   Besides the land in Commerce, much land in Iowa was purchased by the characteristic Mormon method, first by the church, being later sold or given to its members according to their need and financial ability.

At first no attempt was made by the prophet to gather his people to Nauvoo.   They were permitted to locate at will in different parts of Illinois and Iowa.   But in the winter of 1840–41 the legislature of the state granted to the Mormons a very liberal charter.   Under it they were given almost complete political and judicial control of affairs within the city of Nauvoo.   In May following, all the Saints living outside of Nauvoo were called in to help build up the city and its temple.   The call came as a revelation.

And again, verily I say unto you, let all my Saints come from afar,

And send ye swift messengers, yea, chosen messengers, and say unto them: come ye, with all your gold and your silver, and your precious stones, and with all your antiquities; and with all who have knowledge of antiquities, that will come, may come, and bring the box tree, and the fir tree, and the pine tree, together with all the precious trees of the earth; and build a house to my name, for the Most High to dwell therein.[1]

To the Saints this was indeed a divine call.   They were to build a new Jerusalem and a temple like the Temple of Solomon of "fir trees" of "precious stones" and "antiquities."[2]   They responded promptly to the call.   Within a few months the city grew from a population of five thousand to twenty thousand.   It soon became the largest city in Illinois. Hotels and workshops and business houses and enterprises of all sorts sprang into existence as it were in a day.   There were many industrial organizations, not for individual gain, but for the building up of the city.   It was the intention of the prophet to make Nauvoo self-supporting and entirely independent of outside business and industrial life.   A city government was established and also a military organization.   The prophet became mayor of the city and also lieutenant-general of the Nauvoo Legion.

But the effect of this wonderful group solidarity was not long to be expressed in terms of prosperity and city building.   The very factors

---

[1] *Doctrine and Covenants*, Section 124:25–26.   [2] I Kings 5:6–8; 6:21.

which created strong solidarity within also developed a strong opposing group without. Here as in Missouri when the non-Mormons found that they were excluded from all the Mormon enterprises they became suspicious. There was something wrong with a people who were always all for or all against a political measure. Little by little they began to feel that since the Mormons' religious, economic, and political interests were so exclusively Mormon interests that they must be opposed to their own. Joseph Smith, whom the Saints regarded with such reverence, now received the attention also of the Gentiles; by them he was regarded not with reverence but with contempt and hatred. In fact everything that was considered of vital concern by the Mormons became now of vital concern to the gentile group. But what was an object of love to one group was an object of hate to the other and what was regarded with reverence by the one was regarded with contempt by the other.

The attention of both Mormons and Gentiles in Illinois now became centered in the prophet and never before had the latter been more active than during the last two or three years of his life. On one day he would be presenting to his people a new revelation; the next day he would appear before them as head of the Nauvoo Legion. He might one day be under arrest and on trial before a court in Illinois; and the next day announce himself a candidate for president of the United States. The prophet recognized his activity and regarded it as a source of strength. He says: "Excitement has almost become the essence of my life, when it dies away I feel almost lost. When a man is reined up continually he becomes strong and gains knowledge and power; but when he relaxes for a season he loses much of his power."[1]

The prophet was arrested a great many times and each occasion tended to magnify his greatness in the minds of his people. Wilford Woodruff describes a reception the people gave their leader upon his return after a hearing before a court: "Five days later . . . . the citizens of Nauvoo went out in great numbers on horseback and in carriages to meet the prophet. The whole scene was a demonstration of joy. He was escorted home by a band of music and by the great multitude that had gone out to meet him."[2]

Inspired by the presence of thousands of his people and by the glorious reception which they extended him, he gave direct expression

[1] Statement by Wilford Woodruff, quoted by Cowley in *Life of Wilford Woodruff*, p. 176.

[2] *Ibid.*, p. 182.

to his emotions. The following selections from his address reveal his temperament and also indicate his relation to the people:

"I want you to learn, O Israel! what is for the happiness and peace of this city and its people. Our enemies are determined to oppress us and deprive us of our rights and privileges as they have done in the past. . . . .

"There is a time, however, when forbearance ceases and when suffering longer without resistance is a sin. I shall not bear it any longer, I will spill the last drop of blood I have rather than endure it; and all who feel that they will not bear it any longer say, 'Aye'. . . . .

"However, I shall restrain you no longer, from this time forth. If occasion require I will lead you to battle, if you are not afraid to die and to spill your blood in your own defense you will not offend me. Be not the aggressor. Bear until they strike you on one cheek and then offer the other. They will be sure to strike that also; then defend yourself and God will bear you off victorious. If I am under the necessity of giving up our chartered rights, privileges, and freedom for which our fathers fought and bled, and which the constitution of the United States as well as this state grants to us, I will do it at the point of the bayonet and sword. . . . .

"It did my soul good to witness the manifestation of your feelings and love toward me. I thank God I have the honor to lead so virtuous and honest a people, to be your law-giver as Moses was to the children of Israel. Hosanna! Hosanna! Hosanna! to the most high God! I commend you to His grace and may the blessings of Heaven rest upon you, I ask it in the name of Jesus Christ. Amen."[1]

Joseph Smith possessed the essential traits of a prophet. He was highly sensitive to the impulses of his people. This placed him in complete harmony with them. He embodied their spirit and in this sense he was not only a prophet for them but was made a prophet by them. He received his inspiration from the group and in return reflected its life in such a way as to give it restimulation. The group felt the emotions but needed a prophet to make them more objective or give more concrete expression to them. Such emotional expressions as these: "I will spill the last drop of blood I have rather than endure it," "I will lead you to battle," "Defend yourself and God will bear you off victorious," are in a very real sense group expressions. It was the group speaking through its prophet. When the emotions were expressed in this form they became stimuli for even more powerful emotional responses. It is true that the whole life of the people was centered in their prophet, but it is equally true that the spirit and power of the prophet came from the group.

[1] Statement by Wilford Woodruff, quoted by Cowley in *Life of Wilford Woodruff*, pp. 184–86.

The one event which has made the name of Joseph Smith immortal in the Mormon community is his martyrdom in Carthage jail. He was murdered while in the zenith of his life, just at the time when the attention of his entire people as well as his enemy was focused upon him. The time of his death and the manner of his death has established a sentiment in the Mormon people toward him and his enemies that has remained even to the present time and will perhaps always remain as an element in the consciousness of the Mormon people. The following hymn illustrates the nature of this sentiment and the manner in which it is transmitted:

> Praise to the Man who communed with Jehovah!
> Jesus anointed "that Prophet and Seer"
> Blessed to open the last dispensation;
> Kings shall extol him and nations revere.
> 　Hail to the Prophet, ascended to heaven!
> Traitors and tyrants now fight him in vain;
> Mingling with God, he can plan for his brethren;
> Death cannot conquer the hero again.
> 　Praise to his memory, he died as a martyr,
> Honored and blest be his ever great name!
> Long shall his blood which was shed by assassins
> Stain Illinois while the earth lauds his fame.
> 　Great is his glory and endless his priesthood,
> Ever and ever the keys he will hold;
> Faithful and true he will enter his kingdom,
> Crowned in the midst of the prophets of old.
> 　Sacrifice brings forth the blessings of heaven;
> Earth must atone for the blood of that man;
> Wake up the world for the conflict of justice;
> Millions shall know "brother Joseph" again.[1]

In the death of Joseph Smith and the expulsion of the Saints from Nauvoo the first period in Mormon history has its dramatic ending. It is impossible to find a situation which illustrates so well the effect of strong group sentiments. Five times did the Mormons establish settlements and five times were they driven from their homes by mobs. In each place they were kindly received at first, treated as friends, but became after a short time objects of extreme hatred and for no other cause than that they were a peculiar people. We may thus generalize our conclusions of the first great maladjustment in Mormon history. (1) That the extraordinary pretentions of the Mormons which made

[1] Selected from the *Songs of Zion.*

them unpopular among the citizens of Missouri and Illinois were the first cause of the conflict. (2) That the conflict itself created solidarity within the group and prejudice between groups. (3) That the sentiments thus nourished by constant group interaction grew in intensity and resulted finally in mob uprising.

Although the great conflict with the Gentiles practically ended with the expulsion from Nauvoo, its psychological effect still remains and functions vitally in the life of the people. The struggle was too intense and the emotional excitement too great to be quickly eliminated from their consciousness. There is a tendency to rehearse this great conflict in their religious services. The expulsions from Missouri and from Illinois are popular themes for public addresses. In oratorical contests many young Mormons have won prizes with this theme. But perhaps the most common appearance of the mental effect of the great conflict is in the hymns of the church. The following expressions taken from some of the hymns illustrate how dominant is this element of conflict in the consciousness of the people. "All thy foes shall flee before thee"; "Enemies no more shall trouble; all thy wrongs shall be redressed"; "All thy conflicts, all thy conflicts end in an eternal rest"; "All her foes shall be confounded, though the world in arms combine"; "While the enemy assaulteth shall we shrink or shun the fight"; "On the necks of thy foes thou shalt tread."[1] The one element common to all these expressions is that of conflict with an enemy. This is one of the most effective means of transmitting the old group sentiments from one generation to another.

But in addition to the effect on the sentiments, the psychology of group conflict is manifest in a more objective way. It is in the peculiar character of some of the religious forms. They are unlike that of the sectarian world. The Mormons had no inclination to compromise with the outside world. This tendency has grown out of the old classification, the Mormons and Gentiles, the Children of God and the Children of the Devil, their brethren and their enemies. Nothing good can come from an evil source, consequently whatever originated in Mormonism was of God and whatever came from Babylon was of the Devil. It was the peculiarity of Mormonism which caused the conflict. And it was the conflict which caused these peculiarities to continue. There would have been no strife with the gentile world had it not been for Mormon peculiarities and there would have been no Mormonism as we have it today without this conflict. Thus we have in Mormonism peculiar religious

[1] Selected from the *Songs of Zion*.

ceremonies, a peculiar marriage institution, a distinct economic order, and a unique priesthood with its own institution for social control.

But while we are emphasizing the permanent effect of the great conflict in Missouri and Illinois, it is not intended to minimize the significance of the second great struggle. The struggle for existence in the Rocky Mountain country had equally important psychological and social results. We shall observe how the new problems reshaped, changed, and even eliminated some of the older institutions. We shall also observe how the group sentiments of the first conflict were strengthened and how other sentiments developed out of the new life.

PART II

MALADJUSTMENT BETWEEN MORMONS AND NATURE

CHAPTER V

THE MORMON MIGRATION—FROM A CONFLICT WITH MEN TO A STRUGGLE WITH NATURE

With the expulsion from Illinois began the great Rocky Mountain colonization for which the Mormons are so well known. This is the beginning of a new era in Mormon history and marks as well a forward step in American Western movement. Although during the first fifteen years of their history the Mormons were engaged in establishing colonies and building cities—an aim which has characterized their history throughout—the great obstacles were not presented by nature but by their human enemies; the maladjustment was with men. The struggle of the second period was with nature, the economic condition of an isolated mountainous and arid region, inhabited by Indian tribes. It was the successful manner in which the Mormons met and overcame their obstacles that entitles them to a place in the history of the advancement of industrial America.

"To your tents, Oh Israel!" was the command of the new leader who was given the task of directing the Mormons in this pioneering enterprise. Brigham Young became the prophet to the Mormons after the death of Joseph Smith. And it was well that a change of leadership should come at this time. The situation demanded it. Joseph Smith was a spiritual-minded idealist; he seemed to serve the purpose of his group when the conflict was social, religious, and spiritual. Brigham Young was a materialist, very practical-minded and well prepared to direct the Mormons in their struggle with material problems. It seems proper that Joseph Smith should be the founder of a religion and that Brigham Young should be the founder of a state.

Professor Ames in his book, *The Psychology of Religious Experience*, explains the conditions out of which social leaders develop:

The underlying condition is . . . . that of a vital, urgent life for the whole social group. Great men have arisen in crises when the nation or race felt the stress of unusual tension and opportunity. At such times the currents of thought and feeling are deepened and quickened. Not only are the unusual men demanded by the situation, but they are created by it through the stress and stimulation and experience which it furnishes.[1]

[1] P. 344.

We can hardly find a more vivid example of the principle that a new problem forces readjustment than is found in this transition period of Mormon history. The new need created a new type of leadership. The spiritually minded, idealistic leadership gave way to common sense and practical authority. The emotional, inspirational, and impulsive control gave way to deliberative foresight and direction. The loose and incomplete organization was transformed into a more complete, firm, and definite system based upon immediate practical demands.

Brigham Young was once asked if he regarded himself a prophet and replied: "I am of profit to my people." And so he was. As a leader he met the problems confronting his people in such a masterly way that he soon seemed to them a more than ordinary man. He was at first regarded as one of the twelve apostles, the president of the quorum of the apostles. But as his importance to the community became recognized and as the people tended more and more to look to him for leadership, he became clothed with a sort of spiritual sacredness that seemed to lift him into a sphere by himself. He became their "Prophet, Seer, and Revelator."

But what were the problems that demanded this new type of leadership? They were many and varied in character, but they may be summarized under three general economic problems: immigration, colonization, and economic independence. More specifically: (1) How were the thousands of Mormons to be transported from Illinois to the Rocky Mountains? (2) How were they to survive when they got there? (3) In their isolation how could they maintain permanently, as a community, an independent industrial and commercial life? The problems were not all grasped at once by the people. Even Brigham Young was unable to define all of them at the beginning. The problems became organized in the minds of the pioneers while they were struggling with them. We shall treat the problems in the order in which we have stated them for that, in general, is the order in which they presented themselves. But it should be observed that they are not independent of each other. They are in reality three aspects of the one big problem, the establishment of a great and independent Zion in the Rocky Mountain country.

It was on February 4 when the exodus from Illinois actually began, although weeks before this date the people had been engaged in making preparation for their journey. Land and houses were exchanged for cattle, horses, mules, wagons, tents, farm tools, seeds of all kinds, and minor traveling equipment.

The organization for the great journey was very efficient. And it must necessarily have been so in order to move such a great body of people a distance of fifteen hundred miles over trackless prairies, sandy deserts, and rocky mountains. Brigham Young instructed his people thus: "We will have no law we cannot keep, but we will have order in the camp. If any want to live in peace when we have left this place, they must toe the mark."[1] Not all the rules that governed the pioneers were given at any one time but were made as the occasion demanded by Brigham Young and the twelve apostles who represented the church and whose word was law.

The following quotation from a pamphlet published by the historian's office of the Mormon Church in 1869, gives a detailed account of the camp organization and shows the emphasis placed on community interest even at the expense of the individual.

The companies for the plains were organized at the Elk Horn river, about 18 miles west of Winter Quarters, now Florence, Nebraska, into companies of hundreds, fifties, and tens; each fifty was provided with a blacksmith and wagon maker with tools for repairing wagons and shoeing animals. Three hundred pounds of breadstuff were required for each person emigrating, and a good gun with 100 rounds of ammunition for each able-bodied man. Many cows were worked in the yoke. Each family was also required to take a due proportion of seed grain and agricultural implements. Every wagon, load, and team was inspected by a committee, and none were allowed to start on the plains without the required outfit. A strict guard was kept over the cattle by night and day, also in the camps, which were formed in an oval shape, the inside making a corral for the stock. Pigs and poultry were carried in coops attached to the wagons.

No person was allowed by the rules to wander about, not even to hunt game, except under special directions, and by these precautions, no person was lost and but few accidents occurred, and the loss of animals was small, although we traveled ten hundred and thirty-four miles, from the Missouri river to Salt Lake City, through an uninhabited and desert region. Saturday afternoon was usually occupied in washing, baking, repairing wagons, and shoeing animals, and Sunday was a day of rest and worship. Morning and evening prayers and songs of praise were never omitted in the camps, and occasionally a dance was enjoyed, the companies generally being favored with musical talent.

Thus the refining influences of society and civilization were continually felt and kept in view, and the moral status of the camps preserved inviolate through all the fatigues, hardships, exposures, and vexatious annoyances of the entire journey.[2]

This may appear to be a very arbitrary and extremely rigid system, but when we realize the seriousness of the whole situation it should not seem unnecessary. These people were traveling in constant danger of attack from unfriendly Indians and perhaps from some few dissatisfied

---

[1] Quoted in *Tullidge's Quarterly Magazine*, I, 8.   [2] *Answers to Questions*, p. 17.

members of their own group.   They formed a very large body and were
in danger of starvation as well as contagious diseases.   A routine
method and a most rigid discipline were therefore desirable precautions
against serious disturbances.

A most admirable plan, looking to the needs of the Saints who were to
follow the pioneers, was the establishment of farming stations along the
line.   Most of these were located east of the Missouri River where the
rainfall was sufficient to assure a crop.   One was established at Garden
Grove, in Iowa, one-hundred and fifty miles from Nauvoo, another on a
branch of the Grand River, and the largest one at Council Bluffs, on the
Missouri River.   These places were selected by men sent out in advance
of the pioneer wagons.   As soon as the main body arrived at these rest-
ing-places all the men were promptly organized and put to work, some
cutting logs, splitting rails, others building houses and fences, and still
others were engaged in plowing and planting.   Thus industrious settlements sprang up in the wilderness as it were by magic.   In no time of
their experience have they found their communistic scheme quite so
practical as in the conducting of these farming stations.   Thus the
pioneers who reached these stations in the spring would plant the seeds
and the autumn travelers would reap the harvest.

On July 24, 1847, the first pioneers entered Salt Lake Valley.   The
problems of the plains had been successfully met.   And the Mormons
had found a land of peace if nothing else could be said in its favor.   They
were happy in the victory attained but fully realized that a perplexing
problem of a different nature now confronted them.

In order that the reader may fully appreciate the new problem confronting the people and to properly evaluate the methods which Brigham
Young and his associates employed, a few facts are presented.   By the
end of the first summer about four thousand people had entered the
Valley.   They were without surplus food, having brought with them
only sufficient to meet their needs on the journey.   They were practically
without implements or machinery of any kind.   They came from the
fertile lands of Illinois and Missouri and with agricultural knowledge
which, although well suited to the conditions of that country, was entirely
unsuited to the dry lands of Utah.   They had become familiar with the
theory of community enterprise and had even experienced it under
certain conditions but they were not trained in such co-operation as was
required in irrigation, road building, fort building, and other activities
peculiar to the new country.   After the pioneers had been in the Valley
a little more than a year the bishops of Salt Lake wards took an inven-
tory and officially reported that there was little more than three-fourths

of a pound of bread for each person. It is not surprising, therefore, to learn of their eating roots and meat of cattle killed by wolves and even boiling the hides that had been used for roofing the cabins. Some were without clothing and were compelled to cover themselves with the skins of wild beasts when even such could be had.

The psychological effect of these hardships, coming as they did immediately after the persecution in Missouri and Illinois, cannot be overemphasized. The Saints naturally regarded their poverty and misery and the loss of their loved ones as results of the injustice imposed upon them by their gentile enemies. Isolation did not cause them to forget these enemies but, on the contrary, every hardship they endured was a bitter reminder of those who had deprived them of home, of comfort, and of happiness. On the other hand, the thoughtful supervision of Brigham Young and the leaders of the group and the kind helpfulness manifested by the brethren developed a consciousness of Providential care. It is in just such situations of extreme suffering, with the accompanying feeling of dependence upon others for sympathy and assistance, that the Providential Spirit comes to consciousness. At such times the representatives of the group, the prophet, the bishop, the elder, became clearly the representatives of God. Whatever else Providential care may be, it is certainly the spirit of comfort in times of distress.

The great migration was also a splendid discipline for the extensive colonizing enterprises which followed. The careful organization necessary for the moving of such a great body of men, women, and children proved equally efficient in the establishment of numerous small colonizing companies in the mountain valleys. And also the type of discipline which the members of the church received on the plains certainly strengthened the control of the priesthood. The power of church authority was so impressed upon the minds of the Saints during their journey from Illinois to the Great Salt Lake Valley that it tended to remain for years afterward, even when rigid authority was unnecessary and sometimes disadvantageous.

CHAPTER VI

MORMON COLONIZATION

The question of social control was not so perplexing as was that of making a living.   The Saints were anxious to work out their own methods of government.   When they entered the Valley of Great Salt Lake it was Mexican territory, but was ceded to the United States in 1848.   In 1850 the United States government organized the Territory of Utah and appointed Brigham Young governor.   From 1847 to 1857 the political control was left absolutely to the Mormon people.   This was the opportune time for them to try out their social institution.   The priesthood was to rule over Israel.   The old marriage system of Abraham and David could be re-established.   The communistic system and the order of Enoch should demonstrate their practical value.   We shall observe in this and the following chapter the function of these institutions in meeting the new problems.

The problem of colonization presented three aspects: (1) How can the arid country be made to sustain human life? (2) How can the Saints gain possession of all the productive valleys of the Rocky Mountains? (3) How may their population be increased?

1. How to make the arid region produce food to sustain life was by far the most imposing of the many questions that engaged the minds of Brigham Young and his associates.   The Saints had been told by men of experience, traders in the Rocky Mountain region, and by statesmen at Washington, that this vast Mexican territory was valueless and would sustain life in neither man nor beast.   Thus, before entering the Valley, the active minds of the camp were undoubtedly focused on this question.   The possibility of taking water from the mountain streams and distributing it over the dry lands had no doubt been suggested by someone who felt keenly the task of feeding a multitude in the desert, for the very day on which they arrived in the Valley the experiment was made.

While irrigation had been practiced in Egypt for many ages and had been in use in a simple form among some Indian tribes of the Rocky Mountains, it was Brigham Young and the Mormons who gave it a scientific beginning.   The task of constructing canals in a mountainous country and of distributing the water in fair proportion among a community of farmers was an accomplishment as meritorious as any of the scientific discoveries of significance in the industrial history of the country.

But it is irrigation in relation to the great colonization enterprise which concerns us here. In the first place, it was irrigation which made it possible for any large number of people to live in this arid and isolated country at that time. Starvation would certainly have come to the thousands of Mormons had it not been for this most important discovery. The practical demonstration of irrigation made possible a great future for the new country and its inhabitants. Brigham Young could now see in vision the Saints growing in numbers and becoming a "mighty people." He saw them occupying every valley in that great expanse of country. He saw the water of every stream diverted from its natural course to cover the dry lands, making them produce useful crops in abundance. He saw the fulfilment of ancient predictions that Zion should be established on the tops of the mountains and that all nations should flow unto it. This was, indeed, the "Promised Land," and the place where God's Kingdom was to be established.

Irrigation began on a co-operative basis. The task of bringing water, five, ten, and twenty miles through canals cut deep into hard rock, along steep mountain sides and through soil containing roots of trees and brush was not accomplished by a few individuals. It required the united effort of an entire community. This was always taken into account in sending out colonizing companies. The size of the company depended upon the character of the irrigation project that must be undertaken as well as upon the number and size of the streams of water in the locality. When the canals were completed and water was brought to the land there was usually enough for each man to irrigate a garden plot and a ten- or twenty-acre farm. In the construction of the canal each man was expected to contribute his labor and would receive water (water right) in proportion to his contribution. The canals and the streams of water became thus the property of the community.

The social and economic results of co-operative irrigation are significant. The country was settled by colonizing communities rather than by individuals going out by themselves. The individual received the assistance and protection of the community, and the community in its turn was strengthened by his efforts and at the same time avoided the evil of private monopoly of large tracts of land and streams of water. Consequently, there were in Utah, until recent years, very few large farms. Small farms and intensive cultivation was the natural result of the Mormons' irrigation system. This situation has facilitated the development of the beet sugar industry which is now so important throughout the entire Mormon country.

But while co-operative irrigation, small farms, and community life still prevail in Utah, there is now a tendency for large private concerns to buy extensive tracts of land from the government and construct large irrigation canals and reservoirs and to sell the land and the water to the farmers. Thus, we shall see that in the agricultural, as in every other line of economic activity in the Mormon community, the old co-operative community system is giving way to large corporate methods of business control.

2. In regard to the second aspect of the colonization questions, it was the policy of Brigham Young to have his people settle at the earliest possible date upon all the irrigable land in the valleys. He, therefore, hastened to establish colonies in the many valleys of Utah, and in Idaho, Arizona, Colorado, Nevada, and Wyoming. These colonizing projects were called missions, and properly, too, since the building up and the enlargement of Zion was the great social aim. During the general conferences of the church at Salt Lake City, the heads of families would be called to take these missions. These men with their families, under the direction of a bishop or a bishop's councilor, constituted a colonizing company. The bishop had full charge of all the interests of the company. He directed the surveying, plotting, and distributing of the land. He supervised the building of the fort, the construction of canyon roads, canals, fences, and all the co-operative work of the community. He was also the lawgiver and in case of dispute between members of the company, he was chief arbitrator.

The typical method of establishing a colony was as follows: The land was surveyed and plotted into five- and ten-acre lots. These lots were then distributed. The number and size of the lots that each man received depended upon the size of his family. If a man had five wives and each wife had sons old enough to cultivate the land he might receive five times as much land as a man who had but one wife. If a man were a bachelor, he might receive still less land. The writer interviewed an old gentleman who had assisted in surveying and plotting the land on which Ogden City now stands. He thought that due to his valuable service and because he was among the first to settle there, a good share of the choice land would come to him. But how disappointed he was, when the bishop gave him, on account of his being a bachelor, only a small piece of gravel land next to the mountain. The city lots were similarly plotted and distributed. At first the houses were built to serve as a fort but as the community grew larger each man built his house on his city lot. Thus a community of little more than thirty families had its city lots in the central part and the farms and meadow lands on the outskirts. This arrangement was desirable not only because of the social advantages it gave, but because it afforded better protection from Indians.

3. The third aspect of the problem was one of numbers. As an empire builder Brigham Young needed a large population. If the Mormons were to occupy all the valleys of the Rocky Mountains they must become greater in numbers. Two ways presented themselves as means of increasing the population, the one through proselyting and immigration, the other by increasing the birth-rate. Each of these might be presented as a direct religious appeal, the one to "go into the world and gather out the honest in heart" and the other to "multiply and replenish the earth." Both of these from the very beginning of the church have been considered sacred obligations. It was for Brigham Young to make these principles serve in solving his practical colonization problem.

The church began a regular system of immigration shortly after the arrival of the early pioneers. Proselyting had been actively carried on from the time the church was organized and now there were thousands awaiting an opportunity to "gather to Zion." In England and the Scandinavian countries, as well as in the eastern states, there were many converts who were too poor to undertake immigration to Utah. These were all anxious to come and take part in the building up of the Kingdom and Brigham Young was no less anxious to have them come. Although poor, each able-bodied man and woman was an added unit of strength to the great Mormon enterprise, and the poor converts, when once planted in the new country, gained material advantage, for many of them were without homes in their native land. When these people were offered the loan of transportation expenses they were not slow to accept this opportunity to move West. Few there were of the great number who came to Utah in those early days who realized the physical toil required to make new homes in Zion.

The immigration was conducted under an organization known as the "Perpetual Immigration Company." The presidency of the church stood at the head of the organization and directly controlled its operation, but every member of the church was expected to make contributions to it and thus become a member. It was called perpetual on account of a provision that those who contributed were not to be remunerated and those who were assisted were to return the money with interest, thus making it a perpetual and ever-growing concern.   The people were not expected to pay cash but anything of general value, such as horses, cattle, sheep, wagons, grain, and labor, was received as contribution.   The receipt and use of all these things by the company made it possible for nearly every member of the church to render assistance to his immigrating brethren.

The following figures show the immigration to Utah during the time the company was in active operation and they indicate the success of the scheme:[1]

Year	Immigration	Year	Immigration
1849	2,078	1868	3,232
1850	1,612	1869	2,300
1851	1,370	1870	917
1852	760	1871	1,500
1853	2,636	1872	1,631
1854	3,667	1873	2,536
1855	4,294	1874	2,006
1856	3,533	1875	1,523
1857	2,181	1876	1,184
1858	none	1877	1,532
1859–60	2,433	1878	1,864
1861–62	5,556	1879	1,514
1863	3,646	1880	1,780
1864	2,697	1881	2,293
1865	1,301	1882	1,775
1866	3,335	1883	2,460
1867	660		

The company not only paid the immigration expenses and conveyed the Saints across the plains, but it gave them opportunity for employment and directed them in establishing homes when they arrived.   The names of the immigrants were sent to Salt Lake City in advance and posted in public places.   Friends of the immigrating Saints were also notified in order that they might meet them and take them to their homes.   Those who were not otherwise cared for were furnished employment in public shops maintained by the church in the Temple Block.   Others who had had experience in forming colonies and who were financially able were sent out under the supervision of a practical pioneer to colonize a new valley which had previously been explored.

[1] Marcus Jones, United States Treasury Expert, Utah, *Utah* (a pamphlet published in 1890).

The instruction of Brigham Young to one of these companies of newly arrived immigrants makes clear his spirit and method in dealing with the thousands who were thus brought into his domain. The quotation also illustrates the contrast between his practical and direct method of instruction and Joseph Smith's divine revelations.

" . . . . With regard to your obtaining habitations to shelter you in the coming winter, all of you will be able to obtain work and by your industry you can make yourselves tolerably comfortable in this respect before winter sets in. All the improvements you see around you have been made in the short space of four years; four years ago today, there was not a rod of fence to be seen, nor a house, except the old fort, as we called it, though it was then new. All this that you see has been accomplished by the industry of the people, and a great deal more that you do not see, for our settlements extend two hundred and fifty miles south and almost one hundred miles north.

"We shall want some of the brethren to repair to some of the settlements, such as mechanics and farmers; no doubt they can provide themselves with teams, etc., to bear them to their destinations. Those who have acquaintances there will be able to obtain dwellings until they can make accommodations of their own.

"Again with regard to labor; don't imagine unto yourselves that you are going to get rich at once by it. As for the poor there are none here; and neither are there any who may be called rich; but all obtain the essential comforts of life. Let not your eyes be greedy. When I met you this afternoon I felt to say 'this is the company that I belong to, the poor company' as it is called and I always expect to belong to it, until I am crowned with eternal riches in the Celestial Kingdom. In this world I possess nothing only what the Lord has given me, and it is devoted to the building of this Kingdom.

"Do not any of you suffer the thought to enter your minds that you must go to the gold mines in search for riches. That is no place for the Saints. Some have gone there and returned. They keep coming and going, but their garments are spotted almost universally. It is scarcely possible for a man to go there and come back to his place with his garments pure. Don't any of you imagine to yourselves that you can go to the gold mines and get anything to help yourselves with. You must live here, this is the gathering place for the Saints."[1]

But no less important than the immigration of converts as a factor tending to increase the Mormon population and thus hasten colonization was the strong emphasis upon early marriage and polygamy. The origin of the Mormon marriage system and polygamy as the cause of conflict is treated in a following chapter; it is intended here to merely call attention to this system as a factor tending to increase the birth-rate in the

[1] Address of Brigham Young, *Deseret News*, Vol. II (1852).

Mormon community. It is a basic principle in Mormon religion that every matured man and woman in Zion should marry and raise a large family. Bachelors were, therefore, uncommon in early days in Utah and by no means popular. And under the polygamous régime women of the class stigmatized "old maids" were also few. Women entertained suitors from among both the married and the unmarried men and usually made their choice early in life. A few men in that system had as many as twenty-five or fifty children and women ten or twelve children. The following, published in a Mormon journal in 1873, illustrates the situation as well as the attitude at that time toward the subject:

At the close of a two days' meeting held at Springville a gentleman came forward and presented a specimen of the practical results of one branch of co-operation very peculiar in Utah, though rather unpopular in some of the eastern states. This was a fine, straight, four-year-old boy, which the father stated was the tenth child of its mother and forty-fourth born to him since he was forty years old. Such co-operation as that is hard to beat, and is worthy the imitation of good men and women everywhere.[1]

The problem of colonization was thus attacked in a masterly way. The problem of making the arid land produce food was courageously met and solved about as quickly as it was presented. The solution of the most immediate problem stimulated the colonization spirit until nearly every fertile valley in the great Rocky Mountain region supported a small colony of Mormon people. These colonies grew rapidly. The constant stream of immigrants coming in from the east and distributed among the colonies and, on the other hand, the large families were now demonstrating the efficiency of the entire system.

Having thus before us the facts of the operation and efficiency of the Mormon colonization system, what is the explanation? Was it the result of a great genius? Was it a plan carefully thought out by Brigham Young and his associates or was it a sort of chance achievement? Did one man's mind work it out or was it the accomplishment of an entire community of minds?

Our functional point of view will not permit us to regard this as a plan worked out in advance either by one man or by the entire group. The plan was developed in the process of the adjustment itself. Men do not in real life first think and then act; but they act and think at the same time. The Mormons were thrown into the new situation and really had no time to construct plans and formulate aims. The plans were complete and their aim mentally worked out only when the actual

---

[1] *Millennial Star*, XXXV, 430.

work of pioneering was in process. They later had the plans in the form of institutions which in many respects were only hindrances to further progress. The mental equipment as well as the institutions which the pioneers had for use in organizing their new life was the accumulation from the first great struggle. The process of adaptation was that of making this old subjective material meet the new objective situation.

There were some things, however, which had their origin in the first period of Mormon history which did carry over intact into the second period and functioned in the adjustment. There was the strong group sentiment which held the individuals together. There was also the old ideal of building up an independent Zion which gave direction to the activities and at the same time served as a great motive force. It is doubtful whether the great immigration scheme could have been carried out had not this old ideal played an important part. The tithing system which had its origin in the early period also carried over into the new life and functioned as a means of aiding the poor members of the group until they were able to care for themselves.

But the old institutions of the Mormon group at the beginning of their big undertaking were not entirely adequate to the new situation. They were inadequate for such relatively quick and efficient adaptation of the group to the new situation. Only in a very general way do these things serve as material out of which a plan could be formed. Brigham Young and his associates needed direct experience with the new conditions and out of the experience itself developed the plans for direction.

The one condition which, perhaps more than all others, brought about quick and efficient adjustment was that of concentrated attention. The crisis itself brought about a focusing of the attention upon the problem of making a living. This was the essential condition for unified action and successful co-operation. Not one mind but many thousands of minds were active and alert in the presence of the new situation.

There is a tendency to regard the colonization scheme as Brigham Young's plan. This was not the case; the latter was inspired by his group just as much as was his predecessor. He saw visions and uttered predictions just as did Joseph Smith, and they came as did those of the latter from the powerful inspiration of the group. Brigham Young was not the impulsive and emotional type of leader that we find in Joseph Smith. But it does not therefore follow that he was independent of the group. The only real distinction here is that the Great Pioneer responded to a different set of group stimuli. The first Mormon prophet responded to the emotional excitement of his people; the second prophet responded to the practical attitude of his people toward their immediate problem. Nor does the distinction lie altogether in the fact that each man was sensitive to his own peculiar stimuli. The group when in the Rocky Mountains furnished to their leader stimuli entirely different from those which they presented to Joseph Smith. To make this more obvious compare the stimuli which the people of Nauvoo furnished their prophet upon the occasion of his return from trial before his enemies with that furnished Brigham Young by the poor immigrants who came into Salt Lake Valley. This comparison can be made by observing the quotation in this and in the fourth chapter. In each case we may observe that the words were only reflections of the attitude of the group itself. These principles are illustrated in the following chapter.

CHAPTER VII

INDUSTRIAL AND COMMERCIAL CO-OPERATION—THE UNITED ORDER

During a period of nearly twenty-four years (1846–70), from the time they left Nauvoo until the Union Pacific Railroad reached their country, the pioneers were engaged in a desperate struggle with nature. We have observed how effectively the Saints met the problems of their primitive environment through irrigation and carefully organized co-operative colonization enterprises. The present and following chapters will explain further this concerted effort of the Mormons to firmly establish themselves in an independent kingdom. During these many years they had lived in peace with the outside social world. Their isolation had proved to be a safe protection against any serious gentile invasion. But just as the Mormons were beginning to realize a mastery over nature the old enemies put in their appearance in other forms. The rapid extension of the railroad westward gave the Eastern manufacturers an opportunity to send their goods into a new field. Brigham Young and his associates, though they regarded with favor the approach of the railroad, were not unmindful of the new problem which it would present. They realized the advantages that such communication with the outside world would bring; a long period of isolation had made that matter clear. The pioneers knew what it meant to transport large machinery across the plains by ox team and the weeks and months of time it took to bring a company of immigrants to the Valley. But while Brigham Young was conscious of all the advantages which a transcontinental road would bring, he could see also the danger of his people becoming dependent upon the outside business life, thus weakening the independent community life already so well established.

The great Mormon leader was determined to meet the new situation in such a way that the advantages would be enjoyed and the evils avoided. He proposed two great co-operative movements, one for production and another for the distribution of the goods thus produced. The large machines for manufacturing could now be imported by rail. These could be installed in the local communities and operated co-operatively. The articles thus manufactured could be bought by a home co-operative mercantile institution and sold to the people. This home production and exchange should hold absolute monopoly in the local market and thus close the door to the gentile manufacturers and merchants. Let us observe how the scheme operated.

Before this particular co-operative manufacturing movement was undertaken by the church the greater part of the clothing was manufactured in the home. The Mormons lived, in a very real way, in what economists call the household stage of industry. Knitting, spinning, and weaving were going on in nearly every wagon during the entire journey across the plains and continued for many years after the pioneers were established in the valleys. It was practically impossible to buy clothes, and it became necessary to make them in this primitive way or dress in the skins of animals, as many did. Sometimes the hair of wild animals was taken from the hides, made into thread, and woven by hand into cloth. It was the task of the women to make the clothes worn by the family.

The household manufacturing was an extremely slow process which by no means met the demand of a people accustomed to better things. Many of the Mormons came from the manufacturing districts of England and had made and worn better clothing. But what were they to do without the machinery to which they had, through many years, grown accustomed? It was these people who felt most keenly the need of improving conditions and, as the psychologist would state it, experienced a felt need for adjustment, a condition which usually precedes invention. These people, many of whom were iron and wood workers, soon began to create simple machinery for use in supplying some of their necessities. A few small and very necessary pieces of machinery were also brought in from the East by ox teams. At first the houses were built from logs and the lumber for the door and window frames was cut with whip saws and held in place by wooden pegs. But soon the blacksmiths began to hammer out nails. Later sawmills and gristmills were established to serve the larger communities or a group of small communities.

But manufacturing in Utah did not become general until at least three years after the advent of the railroad. The real manufacturing boom came when apparently least favored by economic conditions. It would seem that the time for home-manufacturing was when the Territory was free from eastern competition. But on the other hand it was the railroad which made possible the bringing of larger machinery into the Valley, the condition essential for co-operative home industry.

This was the opportune time to preach the gospel of the United Order, and for nearly five years this system was urged upon the people.

It was preached in every religious meeting; special pamphlets were published by the presidency of the church and sent out among the people; the papers and magazines of the church were filled with discussions of the theory and practice of the system. Two lines of argument were presented: one, that it was the divine order revealed to the Prophet Joseph Smith and that practiced by the disciples of Christ and by the Prophet Enoch; the other, that it would serve a present practical purpose. The possibility of the United Order meeting the social needs was the main reason why Brigham Young advocated it at this time. If he thought that ideals and methods of Joseph Smith were practical he would urge them upon his people but when they proved to be unsuited to conditions he would make such substitutions as he thought proper. Many of his associates were more anxious than he to force into existence institutions that had no other justification than that they were established by Joseph Smith or taught or practiced by biblical prophets. The following statement of E. W. Tullidge made in 1876 illustrates Brigham Young's methods:

In the altered state of things that quickly ensued, Brigham Young met all the conditions. Indeed, so rapid and varied were his transformations during the next few years that he may have often seemed to have been reversing himself and his policies. The fact is he was testing his problems, now urging his social ideas with all the might of his matchless will, now accepting with resignation the degree of progress attained by the people. This has been strikingly illustrated in his efforts to transform the Mormons into the great co-operative community, and to establish in Zion the Order of Enoch.[1]

A few illustrations will show the character and extent of the organization as developed at that time. In some communities it was merely a loose co-operative undertaking, in other places it was highly communistic. In Hyrum, Cache County, for example, the people owned in common the sawmill, the tannery, and the store, but the individuals owned the farms, the houses, and the cattle. In Price, Carbon County, on the other hand, the people lived together as one large family. Their farms, mills, horses, cattle, wagons, houses, and everything except the clothing they wore were owned in common. They all ate at the same table, and the women prepared the food and washed the dishes co-operatively. In Brigham City, the organization included about fifteen departments, each under the management of a foreman who, besides directing the labor, kept the accounts of his department. This institution had a woolen mill, a saddle and harness factory, and a tailor department.

[1] *Life of Brigham Young*, 442–43.

They produced men's suits and fur and straw hats for both men and women. The cabinet department supplied the homes with furniture. Besides these departments there were sawmills, machine and wagon shops, a large dairy, and a cattle and sheep herd. In fact nearly every material good which comes under the name of necessity was produced in this little communistic village. It also supplied other communities with manufactured articles. Most of the surplus goods were sent to Salt Lake City and sold to the Zion's Co-operative Mercantile Institution, which in turn made such distribution among the settlements as was needful.

Through the Mormon system of co-operation and the United Order the manufacturing establishments grew from 533 in 1870 to 1,166 in 1880 and this notwithstanding the railroad transportation facilities with the East and the constant effort of non-Mormon merchants to place eastern-made goods on the Utah market.[1] The explanation of this rapid growth of the manufacturing industry in Utah at that time and its subsequent decline is rendered more obvious when we consider the great co-operative mercantile movement that was promoted at the same time.

The United Order and the co-operative manufacturing institutions were incomplete without the mercantile business. A certain amount of exchange was necessary within the communities and between communities. An organized mercantile institution was necessary to facilitate such business relationships. The most independent system that a community could possibly develop found itself lacking in some things. A tannery and a woolen factory could not be economically established in every community. On account of varied altitude, different degrees of soil fertility, the nearness to good water-power and timber lands, a degree of division of labor had to be practiced among the communities.

Furthermore there were many commodities very much needed by the people which they, with all their diversity of industry, could not produce in Utah. Most of the machinery used in manufacturing had to be imported. The completion of the railroad and the importation and the advertisement of a great variety of eastern-made goods made many people dissatisfied with home-made clothing and notwithstanding the fact that the authorities of the church condemned these commodities as luxuries and the purchasers as vain and worldly, the goods were constantly coming in and were being distributed among the people. Thus since the people would have the eastern-made goods it was advisable for the Mormons to handle the business and enjoy the profits. Moreover it was made clear to the leaders of the church through experience with the gentile merchants that the interest of the private concerns was

[1] Hollister, *The Resources* . . . . *of Utah*, p. 55.

in opposition to the interest of the people. Prices had been higher than was thought necessary. This was not at all in accord with the Mormon economic ideal that the welfare of the whole people should always take preference over the interest of the individual. Brigham Young was determined that his people rather than the gentile merchants should enjoy the benefits of the new conditions.

The Mormon church was thus in 1868–69 brought face to face with a most vital commercial problem. It was a question of subduing or being subdued.

The issue was, Should the church "hold her temporal power or lose it?"[1] Should the gentile money agencies be permitted to exact tribute from the "Chosen People"? As early as 1868, Brigham Young recognized the approaching problem and began to take steps toward the organization of a co-operative system which he intended should completely monopolize all the mercantile business in the Territory. A year later his scheme was completed and there was put in operation a most comprehensive mercantile system entitled Zion's Co-operative Mercantile Institution.[1]

The name of the organization suggests its nature and purpose. It was Zion's institution and was sharply distinguished from private institutions which were of Babylon. In front of every store under the system was the characteristic inscription "Holiness to the Lord." Thus like the United Order it was divine in character. So sacred were these co-operative organizations that those who were directly identified with them entered into a "covenant by re-baptism to be subject to the priesthood in temporal as well as spiritual things. . . . ." In fact all the stockholders of this concern were to be tithe payers.

Besides the large store established in Salt Lake City called the parent institution, there were small branch stores located in all Mormon communities. Besides handling the commodities produced in the local settlement, these small stores would buy eastern goods through the parent institution and sell them to the people. Nearly every man in the local community owned stock in the "Co-op" and consequently, besides feeling a religious obligation to support it, found it to his advantage to do so. And for a few years this institution held a complete monopoly of mercantile business in the small communities.

But in addition to serving as a distributing agent of the home-manufactured goods, the Mormons claim for the co-operative mercantile system three economic results: it lowered the price generally of merchandise, it created and maintained uniform prices, and it distributed the earnings to the people. In 1873, Mr. Clawson, the manager of the parent institution, estimated that during the first four years of its existence

[1] *Tullidge's Quarterly Magazine*, I, 363.

it had saved the people $3,000,000. In 1889, when the institution had had a twenty years' history, we read the following in a Utah magazine:

In the twenty years since co-operation has been established in Utah, its influence for good has been recognized in every part of the Territory. Not only in the distribution of profits among its numerous stockholders have co-operative stores been a benefit, but the public at large have shared in the profits, as the old practice of dealing, which promoted trade to increase the price of an article because of scarcity, was abandoned. People had no longer to pay a dollar a pound for sugar, and equally exorbitant prices for other necessaries and commodities. Goods have been sold at something like uniform rates, at reasonable profits throughout the Territory.[1]

But after ten years the small co-operative stores were not succeeding as well as the parent institution. Many of them had ceased to be co-operative. And while they continued to carry the name and the inscription "Holiness to the Lord," in the minds of many people they were not so "Holy" as they were intended to be. A few successful business men had purchased the stock of those not interested and soon the majority of the stock was owned by a very few, who at the same time enjoyed the monopoly by virtue of its being a church institution. People were beginning to complain and to criticize the system and even the parent institution. This complaint became so general that John Taylor, then president of the church, found it necessary to rebuke the critics. This rebuke is significant, indicating as it does the relation of the church and the priesthood to the system.

. . . . I would make a statement to the Co-op. I have had reports from the North, that some parties who ought to know better had said that the Co-op was no longer a church institution and that it was managed, directed, and controlled by a few monopolists and their operations, which I consider very infamous talk, and especially coming from men who profess to be men of honor. The church, I will here say, holds an interest to the amount of $360,000 and then there are 580 stockholders who are Latter-Day Saints in it, besides the interest which the church holds. And when men make such statements, I consider it infamous and contrary to correct principles, and I should recommend their bishops and the authorities of the church where they live to bring them up for standing and treat them accordingly. That enterprise was started, as was properly implied by the initials of its name. What is it? "Zion's Co-operative Mercantile Institution."[2]

The parent institution has continued to operate but with both Mormon and gentile stockholders. It is no longer regarded as a church institution since Mormons and Gentiles alike are interested. The pay-

[1] *Parry's Monthly Magazine*, IV, 195.

[2] *Report of the Fifth Annual Conference*, p. 74.

ment of tithing is no longer required of the stockholders. While the president of the church is at the head of the institution it can hardly be said to be controlled by the priesthood as such. There are about seven hundred shareholders. The Mormon church is interested but it is not the largest stockholder. More than 25 per cent of the stock is owned by non-Mormons. In 1917 the capital stock was increased from $1,077,000 to $6,000,000 and a conservative estimate of the value of its assets places it above $5,000,000 with liabilities of a little more than $1,000,000 making it the largest mercantile institution in the inter-mountain region.

From 1880 to 1890 is the declining period of all the Mormon co-operative enterprises: colonization projects had been greatly reduced, the many co-operative manufacturing institutions had given way to large private corporations, and the co-operative mercantile system surrendered to the competitive system in which Mormons and Gentiles alike are actively engaged. But though the enterprises themselves have all come to an end their influence remained and is significant. The co-operative agricultural and colonization enterprises were the very means of human existence while the Mormons were engaged in a life and death struggle with nature and all of the co-operative economic enterprises have had important psychological effects. The Mormon group consciousness was influenced as much by this community struggle with economic problems as it was by the struggle with the common human enemies of the Middle West.

The second stage in the life-history of the group thus comes to a close with certain definite results. These results need not be considered here since they are fully treated in the third part of our discussion. But we may observe at this point that it was during this period of Mormon history that most of its institutions took definite form. It was here that the priesthood received its claim to the guidance in all the activities of the people. It was here that the purpose and function of the bishop was most fully realized. He became not only the spiritual advisor, but the captain of the colonizing company and the chief judge and arbitrator among the people. It was here that the prophet was made governor and received his political authority. It was here that the tithing system became permanently established and the church began its business activities. It was in this isolated situation that polygamy was first practiced to any extent and all the Mormon theology connected with family life and eternal progression received a lasting place in its system of philosophy. All these institutions were passed on to the next period and are the sources of the third great conflict to which we shall now turn our attention.

PART III
MALADJUSTMENT BETWEEN NEW THOUGHT AND OLD INSTITUTIONS

CHAPTER VIII

THE INNOVATION OF SCIENCE AND DEMOCRACY

On a psychological basis we may distinguish four Mormon generations. The first generation lived in a period of activity and excitement, of strife and stress. It experienced strong emotions and spiritual manifestations. The second generation lived on the sentiments and traditions created by the first. It too experienced strong group feelings which grew out of the thoughts and influence of the past. Like the first, this class was unreflective, but lived in a world of sentiment. Then comes, thirdly, a generation of philosophers or theologians who take an intellectual attitude toward Mormonism but whose group sentiments are still strong enough to determine their thinking. They have a feeling that Mormonism must be right and they set themselves the task to prove it. Theirs is a sort of rationalism similar to that of the Middle Ages. And finally we have a generation of critics and scientists who seem to sense very little feeling of obligation toward the group but are placing the institutions of their fathers on the dissecting table for analysis. This class is making a demand for greater freedom of thought and discussion and it is this demand which is bringing about a third Mormon crisis. Nearly all of the Mormons of the first generation have passed away but the second and third generations are still strong and it is these two classes on the one hand and the critics on the other that are bringing about the present-day conflict, the maladjustment to which we shall now turn our attention.

The individuals in our present society may come in contact with each other in four important relations, educational, economic, political, and family. If there is lack of harmony in a community it will usually make itself manifest in one or in all of these ways. Within the Mormon community at the present time a conflict is clearly manifest in each of the four relations. In the present and the following chapter we shall discuss this internal Mormon strife.

When the Mormon people had fairly mastered their primitive environment and were well established in their mountain homes this new problem arose. We may regard their first two great problems as external in character, a struggle with another group and with nature. The present is an internal problem. And whereas the preceding conflicts tended toward greater group solidarity, the present is destructive to group life.

When the outward pressure was removed and the community had created an economic surplus, thus giving to some of its members leisure and opportunity for study, individual thought, criticism, and skepticism were given birth. So long as the people were at war with nature and with another society there was no time for personal reflection. So long as the people were engaged with a common enemy the individuals were easily controlled by the authority of the priesthood but when the outer problems failed to demand the attenton of the individuals they began to look into their own institutional life.

The new spirit began to manifest itself in 1869 and 1870, in what was known as the "Godbeite movement." Three young Mormon elders, William S. Godbe, L. T. Harrison, and Edward W. Tullidge, men of ability and education, began the publication of the *Utah Magazine*. They were the first to make literature a profession in Utah. They found, however, that purely literary work in Utah at that time was premature. They consequently devoted a portion of their time to the discussion of what they thought were vital social questions.

In Brigham Young's great co-operative scheme he not only thought it necessary to regulate the prices of the manufactured articles but believed it desirable to determine the wages of labor. He called a meeting of his ecclesiastical associates and it was agreed to reduce the wages generally and to fix the wages for the different classes. The unskilled laborers were to have one dollar a day and the mechanics were to receive one dollar and a half a day. As may be expected the working men began to murmur and to discuss the question of organizing into trade unions. The *Utah Magazine* took up the cause of labor and published an article entitled "Our Working Men's Wages." It was an attack upon the prophet and his social policies, and a dangerous thing because it dared question the wisdom of the "Lord's anointed." Next came an article headed "Steadying the Ark," whose first paragraph illustrated the new point of view and at the same time showed the actual situation as it was then manifesting itself.

There are a few people in our territory, who, whenever an independent idea is expressed on any philosophical or theological subject, immediately call out, alarmed, that the speaker or writer in question is "steadying the ark," meaning thereby that such person is trying to dictate to the church. As if—whether the speaker's intention was so or not—the action of independent thought could by any possibility be dangerous to an imperishable system like ours. It is a fear of having something of this kind said about them that has deterred many a person from expressing conceptions of the truth of which they were assured but which did not happen to tally with popular opinion. The existence of such a fear dwarfs and stunts the intellect as well as the spiritual growth of men; and being contrary to Mormonism which was offered to all as the gospel of free thought and free speech, too, should be broken down.[1]

The journalists next attacked Brigham Young's policy in the industrial development of the Territory. The latter had from the first opposed the opening of the mines. The wisdom of this position cannot well be doubted. To have permitted his people to undertake this industry might have resulted in starvation and would have at least put an end to Mormonism. It is now generally conceded that Brigham Young's agricultural policy is largely responsible for Utah's present prosperity. Had the mining motives been unchecked, that industry would no doubt have been more highly developed than it now is, but the great agricultural resources would have been undeveloped and the state would be unable to support more than one-half or one-third its present population.

But there were many at this period who were anxious to enter this speculative industry and were waiting only for the church to change its attitude. The writers insisted that mining was the industry for which the territory was well adapted and that that alone promised a vast surplus. The people were carrying on business largely by barter and it was argued that what the community needed was money, and that the best way to obtain it was by digging it out of the ground. Whether so intended or not the publication of these articles was regarded as the inauguration of a rebellion against the priesthood. Such liberty could not be permitted. The writers were brought before the High Council for a hearing. The following question was put to the young critics by this ecclesiastical tribunal: "Do you believe that President Young has the right to dictate to you, in all things temporal and spiritual? The reply came that they did not believe that the president had such right but that the

light of God in each individual soul was the proper guide and not the intelligence of one human mind. According to the Prophet and his Apostles this was sufficient cause for excommunication and action was consequently taken. The young men inquired whether or not it was possible for them to honestly differ from the presiding priesthood, and were told that such a thing was impossible, and that they might as well ask whether we could honestly differ from the Almighty.[2]

Whether due to the controlling influence of the leaders of the church or to some other cause the question of the independent thinking and

---

[1] *Tullidge's Quarterly Magazine*, I, 22.   [2] *Ibid.*, I, 32.

freedom of discussion within the church did not become again a disturbing question for a number of years.

Some of the more intellectual leaders of the church had written books on Mormon doctrines but the spirit of these had all been to justify the prevailing point of view rather than to analyze the institutions for the purpose of getting at the truth. Of course there had been men not connected with the church who had taught "heresy" to the youth of Zion ever since the time the church was organized. Men connected with the larger state educational institutions had modestly expressed their opinion on what they regarded to be the "delicate subjects." But these critics were all non-Mormon and the prejudice against those of the other group had always been so strong among the Mormons that very little notice was taken of the criticism. Should any of the youth manifest sympathy toward the new interpretation there were always enough orthodox Mormon preachers and educators to counteract the unorthodox tendency.

But about 1907 a number of young men of Mormon parentage returned from eastern educational institutions, where they had received higher degrees. The study of science, philosophy, sociology, and the higher criticism of the Bible had given them a new point of view. Yet they were regarded as Mormon boys of good character and were employed to teach in the high schools and colleges of the church, the system from which they had been graduated a few years previously. They were also placed in positions of responsibility in other Mormon organizations, intended for religious education. But they were not long to enjoy such confidence. Their frank expressions of opinion on such subjects as the origin of man, the visions and revelations of Joseph Smith, the literal interpretation of the Bible, and other subjects in which the orthodox interpretation had been definitely established soon brought about controversy. The young people under their instruction were quick to detect disagreements between the interpretation which their parents had placed upon these things and that which was now made by their professors. The students were mentally disturbed but were by no means antagonistic toward the new doctrine. It had come, not from gentile teachers, but from their brethren in the church. The new doctrine was carried home to the parents who were much less inclined to view with sympathy the instruction which their children were receiving.

There are many reasons why it is extremely difficult for the Mormon doctrines to be harmonized with the new scientific and democratic conceptions. The more basic doctrines of Mormonism center around such questions as the creation of man, the literal interpretation of the Bible, the authority of the priesthood, the divine and eternal nature of Mormon institutions, God's commandments as absolute moral laws, and revelation through the prophet as the only source of all religious truth. All these questions create friction between the present educational spirit and Mormon orthodoxy.

Should Mormonism accept the evolutionary point of view some of its most sacred doctrinal principles would have to be abandoned. All the rituals and dogma which have grown up about Adam and his mission on earth and the commandment given him to multiply and replenish the earth would become meaningless. The story of the Book of Genesis as well as that of the Mormons' own sacred book, the *Pearl of Great Price*, would become mere fiction. And to regard the latter as fiction would be to deny one of the foundation stones of Mormonism. Furthermore, for the Mormons to accept the evolutionary doctrine of the origin of man would be to deprive themselves of their best argument in support of their conception of God. They maintain that God is like a man except that he is perfect. They prove this by the Scripture which says that God created man in the likeness of his own image. Thus to accept as truth the evolutionary theory requires the sacrifice of the basic principle of Mormon doctrine.

Nor can the orthodox Mormons easily accept the teachings of higher criticism. As already observed one of the demands which brought Mormonism into existence was a desire for a more literal interpretation of the Bible. A great many of its institutions and points of doctrine were taken from the Old and New Testaments. That means of course that they cannot give up the seventh article of their faith which reads: "We believe in the gift of tongues, prophecy, revelation, visions, healing, and interpretation of tongues, etc." To deny that these things took place in ancient Israel and in the days of Christ and still believe the Bible to be the book of God is, to them, an impossibility.

Again the sixth article of their faith reads: "We believe in the same organization that existed in the primitive church, viz: apostles, prophets, pastors, teachers, evangelists, etc." In other words this form of organization is eternal and cannot be changed by the "whimsical notions of men." The divine authority of the priesthood is a very distinctive characteristic of Mormon control. The fifth article of faith is even stronger: "We believe that a man must be called of God by prophecy and by the laying on of hands by those who are in authority to preach the Gospel and administer in the ordinances thereof." All knowledge for the guidance of the church, all interpretation of religious doctrine, all authority to preach and teach the gospel, all commandments from God, must pass through one channel, the prophet or president of the church.[1]

Between this attitude on the part of the more conservative members of the church toward their institutions and the authority of the priesthood on the one hand, and on the other hand the attitude of the social scientists who regard all social institutions in the process of change and who recognize no authoritative control above that of the people, and who find human experience to be the only source of knowledge, there is, obviously, slight opportunity for compromise.

And so it was in the case of the three university professors and the committees representing the general authorities of the church. It was impossible for them to come to an agreement which would make it possible for the young men to retain their positions and at the same time continue to teach what they regarded to be scientific truth! The following account of the investigation is taken from the *Provo Post*, a paper published in the community in which the controversy took place.

An extended investigation was held, at which the utmost freedom and cordiality was extended to the professors, each explaining his attitude with perfect frankness and candor.

As a result of this examination and investigation the committee mentioned above found that the statements of Superintendent Cummings were substanti-

---

[1] President Charles W. Penrose attempts to reconcile the demand for freedom of thought with the requirement that the revelations of the Mormon prophet be considered absolute:

"We don't want to prevent men from thinking. I have heard some of my brethren say, 'Well, do you want to stop men from thinking?' Not at all. Liberty to think and liberty to act upon the thought if you don't infringe the rights of others. Liberty to think, brethren, liberty to read, liberty to have theories and notions and ideas; but, my brethren, it isn't your province nor mine to introduce theories into the church that are not in accordance with the revelations that have been given. Don't forget that. And if any change in policy is to be introduced, it is to come through the proper channel. The Lord said only his servant Joseph should do that while he lived, and then after he died others were to be called to occupy the place, and the key is in the hands of the man who stands at the head, if any change is to be introduced in our church. Don't let us fix our minds too much on the ideas and notions that are called science. If it is really science that they produce, something demonstrated, something proved to be true, that is all right, and there is not a doctrine of our church that I can find that comes in direct conflict or contradiction to the sciences of the times if they are sciences, but a great deal of that which is called science is only philosophy, and much of it speculative philosophy, and these ideas change with the ages, as we can see by reference to what has been called science in times that are past."—Charles W. Penrose, *Eighty-eighth Annual Conference*, pp. 21-22.

ated, and they recommended to the board of trustees of the Brigham Young University, which held its session today in the office of the president of the church, that these professors be required to refrain from teaching doctrines that have not received the approval of the church.

At this meeting of the board it was unanimously resolved that no doctrines should be taught in the Brigham Young University not in harmony with the revealed word of God as interpreted and construed by the presidency and apostles of the church, and that the power and authority of determining whether any professor or other instructor of the institution is out of harmony with the doctrines and attitude of the church was delegated to the presidency of the university.[1]

This action of the general authorities of the church had important results. On the one hand it aroused curiosity and stimulated thought in the minds of many of the young people of the church. They were anxious to know all about those things which the entire priesthood had become so concerned about. On the other hand the treatment which the young professors had received had made it clear to them that these things must not be taught or discussed in the church schools. This resulted in a search for information from those who had little regard for the sacredness of religious institutions. It had also the unfortunate effect of stimulating hypocrisy among young college men and women. Young teachers hesitated to express themselves on important matters of scientific and sociological value for fear of losing their positions and receiving the boycott of the church.

But notwithstanding those facts, the educational institutions, both church and state schools, are the great reconstructive forces in the Mormon community. They are injecting into the minds of the young people of the state knowledge of present social and scientific thought which is having its influence in widening their horizon. The young people are beginning to feel a power within themselves to discover truth, to analyze and evaluate principles of doctrine. They are taught the importance of democracy and the advantages of placing in the hands of the people the right to make and change social institutions as conditions demand.

[1] *Provo Post*, February 21, 1911. The three professors resigned their positions at the Brigham Young University and two of them have since left the state.

CHAPTER IX

THE CHURCH AND BUSINESS

"Institutions," says Veblen, "are products of the past process, are adapted to past circumstances, and are therefore never in full accord with the requirements of the present."[1] The institutions in the Mormon church known as the temporal organizations came into existence when the material interests of the members were largely under the control of the priesthood. But for psychological reasons institutions once created cannot easily be eliminated from social life. The fact that they came into existence and met a community need has made them seem vital. The tithing system as well as business and industrial institutions came into being and developed as results of the Mormon effort to meet material needs. The needs were met but the institutions still remain, causing a maladjustment similar to that between Mormon dogma and science—a conflict between old institutions and present demands.

In pioneer days economic life and the spiritual life of the Mormon community demanded a strong centralized control. The people could not have survived the early persecutions had it not been for the ability of the church to help those who were reduced to extreme poverty. The tithing system and the contributions were found very helpful also in the great colonizing project of Brigham Young. In regard to the financial affairs of the Mormon church three criticisms are now common: (1) that the tithing system is inequitable; (2) that the revenues of the church are controlled by a few of its leaders; (3) that the pecuniary interests rather than the social welfare of the people have become the controlling factor in the distribution of its income.

1. Dr. George H. Brimhall, former president of the Brigham Young University, presents the argument for tithing which is typical among those in the church who feel it their sacred duty to justify all the institutions of Mormonism. He says:

Tithe-paying is the most equitable and natural distribution for public support. Behind it stands the principle enunciated by the Lord Jesus Christ, that "to whomsoever much is given, of him much shall be required." Tithing is an income tax divinely assessed and paid as a free-will offering.[2]

[1] *The Theory of the Leisure Class*, pp. 191 f.

[2] *Tithing* (a pamphlet), p. 5.

This argument does not appeal to the critic who cannot call an income tax equitable which taxes the poor man, whose annual income, let us say, is $1,000, at the same rate that it does the rich man whose annual income is $10,000. The most basic ethical principle of taxation, namely, that the rate should be in proportion to an individual's ability to pay taxes, is here violated. The man with an income of $1,000 who pays $50 in tithing may be depriving his family of some of the necessities of life, whereas the man who pays $1,000 out of his $10,000 income, makes no such sacrifice. His family will still have sufficient food, proper clothing, and shelter. Later the church engaged itself in promoting certain business enterprises which were considered necessary in the community. The machinery for the maintenance of such enterprises thus came into being and has remained until the present time.

The Mormon people are now well established in their mountain homes. Persecution and extreme poverty no longer threaten them. There is also enough private capital in the state or within easy reach to promote any new business enterprise that the future social need may require. The church does not now make a practice of paying the expenses of immigrating the Saints or of feeding them when they arrive. In fact few of the old economic problems now remain and yet the old system still remains and with an increased revenue.

The late President Joseph F. Smith informed us that the "entire tithing of the church in all the world for the year 1914 was $1,887,920. In 1917 the tithing dispersements totaled $2,169,489."[1] Besides the tithing, according to President Smith "enough is received from investments to pay the expenses of the General Authorities and the maintenance of the office of the First Presidency." The amount of the tithing annually received by the church was not made public until very recent years. But owing to the pressure from curious people, whose imagination magnified the amount of tithing received by the church, President Smith gave the information. He says:

I am taking the liberty that has not been indulged in very much but there have been so many false charges made against me and against my brethren by ignorant and evilly disposed people, that I propose to make a true statement which will, I believe, at least have a tendency to convince you that we are trying to do our duty the best we know how.[2]

Although tithing is a free-will offering, the failure to meet this obligation is thought to bring serious consequences to a church member. To

[1] *Eighty-fifth and Eighty-eighth Annual Conference Reports.*

[2] Joseph F. Smith, *Eighty-fifth Annual Conference Report*, pp. 129–40.

the non-tithe-payer, "the doors of the Temple are closed and the privileges of sacred ordinances cut off."[1]   He is considered unfit to partake of the sacrament, for "He that eateth and drinketh unworthily, eateth and drinketh damnation to himself."   And finally "Apostasy is the inevitable end of persistent non-tithe-paying."   Those who will not obey "the law of tithing shall not be found worthy to abide among the saints." To many of the Mormon people these consequences are more terrible than the consequences which may follow the neglect of other financial obligations.   In fact many do, as President Brimhall claims that they should, give first consideration to this obligation.

2. But the power that is exercised by the authorities in the control of the church revenues is more important than is the question of the injustice of tithing.   To sacrifice rights in a democratic society is more serious than it is to suffer the wrongs which a system may impose.   Where a few individuals have complete control of the large and increasing church revenues, and where these individuals obtain their positions by revelation rather than by the election of the people and where removal from office cannot be accomplished through the people's own initiative, we have a situation entirely out of accord with the social and ethical thought of the times.   The late President Smith was conscious of the criticism and justified the position of the church as follows:

The Lord has revealed how this means shall be cared for, and managed; namely by the Presidency of the Church and the High Council of the Church (that is the Twelve Apostles) and the Presiding Bishopric of the Church.   I think there is wisdom in this.   It is not left for one man to dispose of it, or to handle it alone, not by any means.   It devolves upon at least eighteen men, men of wisdom, of faith, of ability, as these eighteen men are.   I say it devolves upon them to dispose of the tithes of the people and to use them for whatever purpose in their judgment and wisdom will accomplish the most good for the Church; and because this fund of tithing is disposed of by the men whom the Lord has designated as having authority to do it, for the necessities and benefit of the Church, they call it commercialism.[2]

The very arguments that he presented to justify the system are the very ones that the critic uses to condemn it.   To say that this method of financial control was revealed by the Lord is to admit that it did not originate from the people; and to say that the eighteen men were designated by the Lord as having authority to dispose of the tithing again

[1] George H. Brimhall, *Tithing* (a pamphlet), p. 4.

[2] *Eighty-second Annual Conference Report*, p. 6.

means that this authority was not given them by the people. The very fact that these men claim the divine right to the control of the wealth of the church makes the situation even less democratic.

But the older members of the church, however, do not raise any question regarding the right of the priesthood in this respect. It is entirely in accord with the traditional Mormon notions that the prophet of God has the right to direct in all matters, temporal as well as spiritual. And then again, while this method is not in accord with the social and ethical thought of the times, it is entirely in accord with the everyday practical economic relations. In business and industrial life, absolute control is in the hands of the relatively few; the great majority of the people have no voice in such matters. It should also be observed that, excepting those who have come in contact with the new social and ethical spirit, the Mormon people are not inclined to favor innovations of any kind. The great majority are rural people and naturally conservative. There are very few members of the Mormon church who belong to disturbing industrial organizations or labor unions. The church has always opposed the affiliations of its people with organizations not under its own control, and consequently a very few Mormons have become identified with labor movements.

3. What are the social and psychological effects of this system and how are these results brought about? It is with the community as with the individual: when the economic necessities are provided for, what is left over is spent in luxuries. These nonessentials may take many different forms and are relative to the stage of civilization as well as to the interests and values which a community may have developed. A community may have developed a certain class of spiritual values which it deems highly essential but which another community may regard as unimportant, and, considering the effort spent in acquiring them, even a positive waste of time and energy. There is, for example, in the Mormon church considerable time and money spent in constructing and maintaining temples in which hundreds of people are engaged every day performing sacred ordinances "for the living and the dead." Considerable money and energy is spent in maintaining theological seminaries. To the non-Mormon these are real wastes but to the orthodox Mormon they are among the most important activities of the church. From the social point of view these things must be considered as of secondary value, i.e., they are acquired interests which should be satisfied only after the primary needs have been met. And while these activities were carried on to a limited extent in the early history of the church they have

received their greatest prominence during the last twenty years. In the early days of the church the tithing was used for buying land and for building canals and factories and for the immigrating of the Saints. But there is no longer a demand for this type of enterprise and consequently a large part of the tithing is spent in satisfying "spiritual interests."

But this is not to imply that the church is no longer engaged in business activities. The church owns stock in a number of corporations which it helped to establish in early Utah history and which have become very large and prosperous institutions. It has also investments in new enterprises. The motive now, however, is pecuniary rather than social. It invests its money for profit and not because the community is in particular need of the assistance of the church in promoting business interests.

The income from these investments pays the salaries of the general church authorities, who thus naturally become interested in promoting the business from which they receive their income. This explains why some of the apostles become active business men and adopt the business men's point of view.[1] Other high church officials were prominent business men before they received their church appointment and were selected in part because of their business ability. Joseph F. Smith, while president of the church, was president of the Utah-Idaho Sugar Company, of Zion's Co-operative Mercantile Institution, of the State Bank of Utah, of Zion's Savings Bank and Trust Company, of the Consolidated Wagon and Machine Company, of the Inland Crystal Salt Company, of the Beneficial Life Insurance Company, and of other companies which need not be named. This serves to indicate the great variety of his business interests. In some of these neither the president of the church nor the church itself owns very much stock, but the name of the president of the church attached to a business concern gives it prestige among the Mormon people and creates an attitude of confidence toward it. Charles W. Nibley, the presiding bishop of the church, was for many years manager of the Utah-Idaho Sugar Company. He is one of the most successful business men of the state. Heber J. Grant, now president of the church, and Reed Smoot, an apostle and United States Senator, are also active business men, with the business man's point of view. The other members of the quorum of twelve apostles as well as the presidents of

---

[1] That the Mormon church has through its leaders become strongly pecuniary is not to imply that social interests are entirely neglected or that the officials are using the church to promote their own financial interests. They are men of moral character and business integrity.

stakes are, as a rule, of the business class but are less prominent. Thus the most influential men of the Mormon priesthood are business men and as such place high value upon pecuniary ideals and methods.

This pecuniary point of view which has developed among the authorities of the church is criticized not only by some of the younger members of the church who find it out of harmony with their growing democratic ideals, but also by the older members of the church, who live in rural districts and have not kept pace with this developing business spirit, holding still to the old co-operative and communistic notion of the pioneers.[1] The latter especially are inclined to question some of the business attitudes of their leaders. For example, Hotel Utah, one of the most magnificent buildings of its kind in the country, was constructed through the efforts of the church and its leaders. Many of the people who come to Salt Lake City only once or twice a year for the purpose of attending the general conferences of the church cannot afford to buy accommodations in Hotel Utah. Coming from rural communities they are naturally conservative and inclined to hold to the traditional notion that the church should promote the interest of Zion and her people. They are unable to understand why the tithing which they paid should go toward the construction of such an institution which only the wealthy Gentiles can enjoy. Also, before prohibition went into effect this hotel maintained a bar. Why should the Saints contribute their means to the erection of a building in which liquor is sold? This criticism became so common that the late President Smith took occasion to refer to it in general conference.

We have helped to build one of the most magnificent hotels that exists on the continent of America, or in the old continent either. I am told that it is equal to any in the world in its facilities for convenience and comfort for its guests, for sanitation, for its situation, and architectural beauty, and in many other ways. Well, some of our people have thought that we were extravagant. I would like you to turn to the book of *Doctrine and Covenants* and read the commandment of the Lord to the Prophet Joseph Smith in the city of Nauvoo. The people were requested to contribute of their means to take stock in this building, Nauvoo House, and they and their children after them, for generation to generation, should have an inheritance in that building, for it was intended for the beauty of the city, for the glory of the stakes of Zion, and to accommodate the stranger from afar who came to contemplate the doctrine of the church and the work of the Lord. . . . .

Now I hoped and I prayed and I voted and did all I could in the hope that the good people of this city would vote it dry so that we would not be com-

[1] Heber Bennion, *Gospel Problems*, p. 36.

pelled to allow a saloon or bar to be operated in the Hotel Utah. If you had voted it dry we would not have had any bar there. . . . .

But it went wet and therefore the people that visit us want something to wet up with once in a while, and unless it is provided for them they will go somewhere else and instead of beholding and viewing the beauties of Zion they will go where they will see everything that is not beautiful. . . . .[1]

The hotel was thus built, according to President Smith, "for the beauty of Zion, to accommodate the stranger from afar." But the more humble country folk were unable to comprehend the new standard by which Zion is judged or to see in this representation of pecuniary strength a true symbol of Mormonism. They had looked upon the humble elder, traveling without "purse or scrip" and preaching without pecuniary compensation, as a true representation of the gospel. And it was obvious to them that the "stranger from afar" who could afford to visit Hotel Utah and who is attracted to the hotel because of the bar is not the type of man who would be likely to become a member of the church. The class of people who would be impressed by the display of pecuniary power do not "come to contemplate the doctrine of the church."

Thus the business man's standards and point of view is rapidly developing among the leaders. There is a growing tendency to take sides with the capitalist class and with large corporations against the laboring classes. The philosophy of the church leaders was at one time radical and socialistic; it is now conservative and capitalistic.[2] They do not hesitate in their sermons and in the editorial columns of the official papers to denounce socialism and trade unionism as anarchism when those become active in opposing the interests of business corporations. The present economic order is accepted by them as right and proper. In fact their philosophy seems to have completely changed in this respect from that held forty years ago. The United Order is as far from their minds as is socialism from the minds of the owners of large corporations.

[1] *Eighty-second Annual Conference Report*, p. 30.

[2] President Smith disapproved the tendency to criticize corporate interests. "Let us please fail," he said, "to find fault with industries which are instituted in our midst for the purpose of giving the people prosperity and advancement . . . . or help to build up Zion. . . ."—*Eighty-second Annual Conference Report*, p. 10.

CHAPTER X

CONFLICTS IN THE MORMON MARRIAGE INSTITUTIONS

No institution or doctrine in the Mormon church is regarded as more important and no ceremony is performed with greater reverence than is the Mormon marriage. It is performed in the most sacred of places and by persons possessing the greatest authority. The covenants and vows made on this occasion are the most binding, and grave spiritual consequences are supposed to follow the breaking of them; on the other hand, the greatest blessing that can come to a young couple is to be married in the temple by proper authority for "time and all eternity." According to the Mormons, proper marriage is the first step that a man takes toward the creation of his eternal kingdom, the highest ideal in the mind of an orthodox Mormon.

There is perhaps no relationship of life which is so universally regarded sacred as that of marriage. From the most primitive tribes, of Africa and Australia, to that of the most cultured people of Europe and America, the marriage ceremony is conducted with some degree of reverence. It is only within relatively recent times and among civilized people that the contract conception of marriage is taking the place of marriage as a sacrament. And in the minds of many sociologists this transition is not always accompanied by moral advancement and social stability. According to Ames, marriage becomes a sacrament in primitive life because of its relation to the reproductive process.

Among primitive people the gods were the givers of life and of material blessings, including the young of the flocks and the children of the family. The gods were the gods of fertility, of reproduction. All agencies and processes of this reproductive life were sacred. The sexual organs and the sexual acts were sacred, and they were accordingly consecrated by religious ceremonies. The very antagonism which some claim to discover between developed religion and the sexual instinct is due to the fact that religious customs tend to regulate and thereby preserve and idealize the instinct. Any ascetic tendencies in developed religions are more than offset by the scrupulous, sympathetic regard for the reproductive life, which is expressed by making marriage a sacrament, circumcising or christening the infants, conceiving the deity as father and exalting motherhood in worship and art.[1]

[1] Ames, *The Psychology of Religious Experience*, pp. 221-22.

Thus not only do the Mormons consider marriage as sacred, but primitive and civilized peoples everywhere tend to view sex relationships as sacred and to make the religious ideals center around the sex life. What is the explanation? So far as psychology can account for this it lies in the fact of attention. Anything which frequently attracts the attention will little by little receive importance in the scale of values. If a thing receives attention from the entire group, and for many years it takes upon itself an element of mystery which inspires more than ordinary regard, it becomes an object of reverence. In fact out of the sex instinct develop the highest ideals, religious and moral, that the race has attained.

Professor Thomas attaches great importance to the socializing function of the sex instinct:

This sex-susceptibility, which was originally developed as an accessory of production and had no social meaning whatever, has thus, in the struggle of society to obtain a hold on the individual, become a social factor of great importance, and together with another product of sexual life—the love of offspring—it is, I suspect, the most immediate source of our sympathetic attitudes in general, and an important force in the development of the ideal, moral, and aesthetic side of life.[1]

But besides the powerful instinctive force of sex life to attract the attention of the individual and the social group, attention to sex relationships is also artificially stimulated by ceremonials and formalities that have grown up unconsciously and which now exercise an influence by themselves. The younger individuals in the group are in this way compelled to focus their attention upon that which is made so much of by those around them. They imitate readily; first, the outward expressions are evident, but soon out of the expression a sentiment in accord with their conduct is developed.

The young people frequently hear long discourses on the importance and sacredness of marriage and the blessings of large families. They observe the building of temples and are encouraged to make contributions to their construction. They hear their parents tell of traveling hundreds of miles in order to receive the blessing of marriage in the sacred buildings. Curiosity is awakened by the taboo placed upon the discussion of the sacred rites performed in the temple. All this talk about marriage and preparation for marriage combined with the instinctive interest in sex life have made this relationship the most sacred in the Mormon community.

Before considering the elements of conflict now active in breaking up this sacred and orthodox notion of marriage relationship a brief

[1] *Sex and Society*, p. 120.

statement of the origin and history of this, the most basic Mormon institution, is necessary. Like every other institution and doctrine in Mormonism, the traditional element, brought in contact with modern conceptions, has occasioned conflict. A maladjustment existing between the accumulations of the past and the demands of the present has caused contention within the Mormon ranks.

The ideal form of marriage, according to orthodox Mormonism, is that which was practiced by the ancient patriarchs of Israel. Abraham, Jacob, Moses, David, and Solomon practiced polygamy, and since the God of Israel approved of their lives, and since he is the same yesterday, today, and forever, why, they argue, should he not sanction polygamy among his favored people in the present age? The orthodox Mormon cannot conceive of God's plan as changeable and relative, it must be universal and absolute. They admit of progress in the human race and they preach eternal progression as the essence of God's universe, but the condition of progress they state in absolute terms. For example, there is no progress outside of the bonds of the "celestial order of marriage." And the degree of progress that is made in eternity depends upon the size of a man's family. Polygamy is, therefore, an important condition of progress and a basic principle in Mormon theology.

But it is not enough that a principle was practiced in ancient Israel; before it can be accepted as a part of Mormon doctrine it must be supported by modern revelation. Thus on July 12, 1843, when Joseph Smith was contemplating the marriage form of ancient Israel, he received the revelation which has so profoundly influenced Mormon life. The following are extracts from the revelation:

"Verily, thus saith the Lord, unto you, my servant Joseph, that inasmuch as you have inquired of my hand to know and understand wherein I, the Lord, justified my servants Abraham, Isaac, and Jacob; as also Moses, David, and Solomon, my servants, as touching the principles and doctrine of their having many wives and concubines: Behold! and lo, I am the Lord thy God, and will answer thee, as touching this matter.

"Abraham received concubines, and they bare him children, and it was accounted unto him for righteousness, because they were given unto him and he abode in my law; as Isaac also, and Jacob, did none other things than that which they were commanded. David also received many wives and concubines, as also Solomon and Moses, my servant, as also many others of my servants, from the beginning of creation until this time and in nothing did they sin save in those things which they received not of me."[1]

While the Saints were in Nauvoo, polygamy was not publicly preached. Joseph Smith taught it secretly to some of his associates but not until August 29, 1852, was the revelation presented to the church.

---

[1] *Doctrine and Covenants*, Section 132:1, 37.

From that date until 1890 polygamy was taught and practiced in every settlement in the Mormon country.

The Mormon isolation in the West was most favorable for the establishment and growth of polygamy. There were here only two influences directing the lives of the individuals, the thought and institutions of the Mormon church and native human instincts. Both factors favored plural marriage. On the one hand it was encouraged as ancient custom, as a revelation from heaven, and as a means to a great posterity; on the other hand the fickleness of the sex instinct favored it. The only reason, says Professor Thomas, why monogamy is practiced today is because it has become an acquired habit by the race and "not because it has answered more completely to the organic interest of the individual." When the instinct is thus not only set free from social restrictions and conventional influences, but is actually encouraged by the only social institution now influencing the individual, it is not surprising that the members of the group so quickly accepted the new order of marriage.

For a period of thirty years (1852–82) the polygamous institution was permitted to run its course. It was difficult for the United States officers in Utah to handle the situation. The laws were inadequate and the enforcement of the laws was a still greater problem. But in March, 1882, the Edmunds Bill was passed by Congress punishing polygamy by disfranchisement, imprisonment, and by declaring the children of such marriages illegitimate. This law the government officials in Utah were determined to enforce. Hundreds of men were imprisoned and many more driven to hiding in remote places; women and children were left unsupported and unprotected. Many deaths resulted from the hardships they were compelled to undergo. President Wilford Woodruff wrote in his daily journal, while in hiding: "There has never been a time since the organization of this church when such a universal howl was raised against us. The whole land is flooded with lies against the people of God. The government seems determined on the destruction of the faithful Latter-Day Saints."[1] It was at this time that President John Taylor died and his successor, while still in hiding, writes of him: "President John Taylor is twice a martyr. He was shot four times in Carthage jail when Joseph and Hyrum were slain and there he mingled his blood with the martyrs. . . . . Now in 1887, driven into exile by the United States officers in consequence of his religion, he lays down his life for the truth."[2]

In 1890, partly as a result of the vigorous prosecution of the law against polygamists, but mainly because there was a possibility that

---

[1] Cowley, *Life of Wilford Woodruff*, p. 538.   [2] *Ibid.*, p. 560.

Utah might obtain statehood, the president of the church issued the "manifesto" in which he declared officially that the Latter-Day Saints are "to refrain from contracting any marriage forbidden by the laws of the land." This statement is significant because it marks the beginning of a new era in Mormon history. The United States officers ceased to harass the Mormon priesthood and polygamists. Soon Utah received statehood, and peace and good will seemed to be at once established between Mormons and Gentiles. Polygamy did not discontinue as quickly as the government officers and the people of the country had hoped that it would, but the conflict was made to shift from that between the Mormons and Gentiles to a conflict within the church itself.

On the basis of their attitude toward polygamy the Mormon people are divided into four distinct classes: (1) There is a young radical class who believe neither in the principle nor practice of polygamy, and who believe that it should be eliminated from the church in both root and branch. This is the growing attitude among the young men and women of education in the church. (2) There is also another class of Mormons who believe in polygamy but not in its practice at the present time. They interpreted the manifesto to mean that men who had plural wives at the time that it was issued should cease to live with all but one of them. There were a few men in the church who thus broke up their families after the issuing of the manifesto. (3) A third class, and perhaps the great majority of Mormon people, believe in the principle of polygamy and in its practice to the extent of maintaining the marriages solemnized before the manifesto, but they do not believe in contracting plural marriages after the manifesto. This is the attitude that is taken by the present authorities of the church. (4) A fourth class is also found in the church who believe that neither the government nor the church has the right to eliminate an institution divinely established. This is perhaps the most consistent orthodox class. There are a few men in the church who believe that they have the authority to solemnize plural marriages, and consequently a few such marriages have been performed since the issuing of the manifesto. A large percentage of the polygamists of this order have been excommunicated from the church.

This internal strife is thus a very complex affair. It is not only a conflict between the orthodox and the unorthodox but a contention between the orthodox polygamists themselves. But the one which need concern us here is the struggle going on between the radical and unorthodox members on the one hand and the conservative and orthodox on the other. There are important conditions which tend to keep these two factions actively at war.

We have already observed the main reasons why the orthodox Mormon element cannot easily give up the polygamous doctrine. (1) It was divinely revealed and taught by the prophet as a sacred marriage relationship accepted by God from the beginning of time. (2) Many of the leading men of the church had plural wives and to break up the family would mean great suffering on the part of the women and children. They had already made great sacrifice for what they regarded to be a sacred marriage relation and now to be disowned by husband and father seemed unfair and inhuman. (3) Again, polygamy is regarded as the means whereby the great ideal of the kingdom, here and hereafter, is realized. Says President Woodruff:

> The reason why the church and Kingdom of God cannot advance without the Patriarchal Order of marriage is that it belongs to this dispensation just as baptism for the dead does, or any law or ordinance that belongs to a dispensation. Without it the church cannot progress. The leading men of Israel who are presiding over stakes will have to obey the law of Abraham or they will have to resign.[1]

President Taylor said: "If we do not embrace that principle soon, the keys will be turned against us. If we do not keep the same law that our Heavenly Father has kept we cannot go with him." And (4) finally it was polygamy for which they had for nearly half a century endured persecutions. The very fact that it had required sacrifice magnified the importance of the institution in their minds. It had become the one phase of their religion which created discussion when all other points of doctrine passed into oblivion. It absorbed the attention and thus became the most sacred institution in the Mormon religion.

But there are also forces at work which tend in the opposite direction. The strong emphasis which is now being placed upon evolution in the high-school and college courses of the state is causing the young people to realize that the doctrines of their religion are in process of change. The orthodox class claim that the social institution is absolute and eternal. This does not appeal to the young people, who are interpreting the notions and institutions of the past as products of social conditions then prevailing. Polygamy might have been the most desirable form of marriage among the patriarchs of ancient Israel when the ideals and mode of life were quite different from those which now prevail, but to reintroduce the old institution is too radical a departure from the present standard to be uncritically accepted by the educated young people of the church.

Again, the ideal of a large family does not appeal to the younger Mormon generation with the force that it did to the pioneer fathers.

---

[1] Cowley, *Life of Wilford Woodruff*, p. 542.

The economic conditions are such that parents cannot now raise a large family and maintain the standard of living which present society demands. It is a greater tax on human energy to raise a family of three children under present conditions than it was to raise a family of six children in early Utah days. Again the great variety of opportunities open to those who have a sufficient income along all lines of education attract the attention of the young people away from the old family ideal.

There is also at the present time a tendency toward free social intercourse between the children of Mormon and gentile parents. The old prejudices are breaking down and the non-Mormon influence is being more directly felt. In fact there is an increasing number of marriages between Mormons and Gentiles and a relatively decreasing number who are each year married in the temples of the church. This situation is keenly felt by the older members of the church. Parents who have sincerely believed all their lives that marriages within the church and in the temples are the only marriages which God recognizes find it extremely disappointing to see their children treat this sacred matter with indifference.

And finally, the independent attitude of the young women in Utah would prevent the continuance of polygamy even though the government and the church favored its practice. Due to economic and social conditions, women in Utah, in common with their sisters everywhere in the civilized world, have developed an independence of life which would make such an institution today impossible. While the Mormon people have generally given woman as much freedom as she has enjoyed elsewhere in the country, the philosophy of polygamy has in many cases led the men to regard her as little more than a means of bringing children into the world. When man's glory is stated in terms of posterity, the value of woman to him lies in her power to thus contribute to his glory. The sentiment of woman today is such that she will not thus sacrifice her personality and especially does she object to the sharing of her husband's affection with another woman.

The very institution which caused strong prejudice and persecution from without in early Mormon history is now causing dissension within; the same force that created group solidarity is now destroying it. The institution of polygamy maintained itself so long as it met with strong opposition outside of the Mormon group and so long as the native instincts and Mormon institutions controlled the individual within the group, but when the external pressure was removed and educational opportunities developed a variety of values and interests within the community, the institution of polygamy began to crumble; and before long it will cease to be a problem in Utah.

CHAPTER XI

THE ETHICS OF MORMONISM

The laboratory for ethical study is the field of human history in all of its aspects—political, economic, and religious.   The unit is the social group in the process of its evolution.   All forms of social control, whether in the nature of sentiments, customs, laws, or divine commandments, have their origin in active social life.   In the development of moral standards every human instinct, every interest, every problem which has concerned the community, whether inherited from the past or imposed by the environment, has had its effect.   The meaning and significance of moral standards can be ascertained only by a study of their origin and function in a concrete, active social process.

The life-history of the Mormon group furnishes suitable material for such a study.   In the first place the group has developed in almost complete isolation.   This makes the task of singling out the factors which have determined its moral standards relatively easy.   In the second place the Mormon group has been subjected to very frequent and radical changes in its environment.   These conditions have occasioned readjustments which are significant not only from the social and psychological but from the ethical point of view.   A transition from one social stage to another reveals certain aspects and principles in human life which would not be noticed under less active social conditions.   And, thirdly, we have here the complete life-history of a group.   We are thus able to view the moral standards in relation to their origin, their function, and their termination.

The moral concepts in Mormonism have developed out of vital group experiences.   Thus to give a satisfactory account of them we must consider them in relation to the three great Mormon crises.   Our discussion thus divides itself into three parts: (1) The group morality of the Mormons as the result of their conflicts with the non-Mormons of Illinois and Missouri.   (2) The practical and materialistic ethical conceptions which developed out of the economic struggle in the Great Basin.   (3) The present theological ethics considered as the crystallization of older group sentiments and ideals.   These three stages in Mormon ethics correspond, to a certain degree, with three common ethical points of view.   The attitude in the first stage resembles that of the sentimentalist, conceiving morality as a feeling attitude. The second stage is essentially the utilitarian attitude. The material welfare of the community seems to be the ethical criterion. In the third stage we have a sort of casuistic attitude. Morality is here regarded as a matter of adhering to a code of rules or commandments.

Although the concrete material presented in this chapter is selected to illustrate what is essentially peculiar to the Mormon ethical life and to each of the three stages in their ethical development, it should not be inferred from this that the general moral standards and ethical notions of the Mormon people are essentially different from those of other people or that there is an absolute difference between the moral attitudes of the three levels in Mormon moral evolution. There are more similarities between the Mormon and non-Mormon ethics than there are differences; and so also there are more similarities between the three stages than there are differences. However, the fact that there are differences, whatever the degree may be, is still significant and presents a real problem. Our effort is to make clear these distinctions and give an explanation for them. The material selected and the method employed should do this without at the same time conveying the false impression of absolute distinctions. While there are variations in the moral standards of different groups and within social groups there is also unity and continuity without which differences would have no meaning.

Before entering upon the main problem of this chapter it is necessary to state briefly the psychological premises of our discussion. It is here maintained that the moral self is essentially social and that the individual becomes conscious of moral values just as he does of every other class of interests through a process of action and reaction with the other members of his group. Our second proposition is that the moral sentiments of Mormonism are mainly group sentiments, simple and intense in the first stage but developing through the problems of the second and third stages into a more complex system of group control. These group sentiments are personified in the God of Israel. He is the embodiment of the moral concepts of the group. Although these principles have been sufficiently demonstrated in previous chapters and may here be regarded as premises of our discussion, yet their direct application in this connection will more fully establish their validity.

I

The first period in Mormon history, the period in which Joseph Smith was prophet to the group, we have already characterized as that of great excitement and intense emotional experiences. It was the period of visions and revelations. Practically all the revelations that were ever given to the church came at this time. It was the time of miracles, or prophecies, of signs and wonders. It was the time when "whole villages" were converted in a day and hundreds apostatized at the same time.[1] It was the period of uncertainty, of instability. Psychologically, it was the stage of alternate joy and sorrow, of great love and intense hatred. It was the initial stage of Mormonism, when the group was being formed and its attitudes established.

We have pointed out in previous chapters how the Mormons appropriated both the name and the traditions of ancient Israel; and how this imitation of ancient ceremonies and of Bible language, and the claims to revelation and divine authority, tended to create prejudice and persecution against Joseph Smith and his followers. Out of this conflict developed, as we have observed, the Mormon group spirit. We shall now see how this group spirit affected the moral attitude of the people. The revelations and sermons and literature of this period clearly reflect the moral sentiments.

We have here the characteristic traits of group morality. All people outside of the group were enemies and all within the group were brethren. The God of Israel was the God of Mormonism and the devil ruled over the Gentiles. "The devil shall have power over his own dominion," says the revelation, "and the Lord shall have power over his Saints and shall reign in their midst and shall come down in judgment upon. . . . the world."[2] And again, "Let all the Saints rejoice, therefore, and be exceeding glad, for Israel's God is their God and He will mete out a just recompense of reward upon the heads of all their oppressors."[3] These were not simply the expressions of Joseph Smith. They were the sentiments of the group. They expressed the spirit which transcended the life and spirit of any one individual. The God of Israel, the spirit of the group, was speaking.

God was on the side of the Mormon group and would punish all who rebelled against the chosen people. "And the rebellious shall be pierced with much sorrow" and he who will not hear the voice of the servants of God "shall be cut off from among the people" and "shall perish in Babylon, even Babylon the great shall fall."[4] But, on the other hand, observe

[1] O. F. Whitney, *Life of Heber C. Kimball*, pp. 181–93, 194–99.

[2] Joseph Smith, *Doctrine and Covenants*, Section 1: 35–36.

[3] *Doctrine and Covenants*, Section 127: 3.

[4] *Ibid.*, Section 1: 3, 14, 16.

the sentiment toward the Mormon group. "Therefore, fear not, little flock, do good, let earth and hell combine against you, for if ye are built upon my Rock, they cannot prevail."[1] And again, "Awake! O Kings of the earth! come ye with your gold and your silver, to the help of my people, to the home of the daughters of Zion."[2]

These expressions, while imitative of Old Testament prophets, did reflect the Mormon group spirit. In fact the Mormons regarded themselves as belonging to the Israelitish group and of the same blood. And all who are of the blood of Israel are favored of God but the "rebellious are not of the blood of Ephraim, wherefore they shall be plucked out."[3] This enlargement of the group to include ancient Israel gave strength to the group sentiments. The tribal God of ancient Israel and the animosity which Israel held toward other tribes seemed to correspond to the spirit of Mormonism at that time and was easily taken over into its own group life.

Group morality was also shown in dealing with the members of the group. The great sin was disloyalty. This was a sufficient cause for excommunication. The following cases are illustrative: W. W. Phelps and John Whitmer were severed from the church for "selling their lands in Jackson County" and thereby setting "an example which all the Saints were liable to follow." To sell their inheritance in Zion "was a hellish principle, and. . . . they had flatly denied the faith in so doing."[4] David Whitmer was excommunicated for "leaving or forsaking the cause of God, and returning to the beggarly elements of the world, and neglecting the high and holy calling according to his profession."[5]

It was this bitter group antagonism which gave birth to the sentiment of fellow-feeling and brotherly love which is so characteristic of the Mormons, especially during their early history. It was a despised enemy which made them conscious of their beloved brethren. The fact that the entire group focused its attention upon the enemy was the essential condition for sympathy within the group. It was the common object of hate which conditioned the common object of love. The individual becoming so completely merged into the activity of the group lost consciousness of personal interests. His entire life became identified with his group. The self was a group self; it was made up of the combined interests of all the brethren. When they suffered he suffered in a very

[1] *Ibid.*, Section 6:34.

[2] *Ibid.*, Section 124:11.

[3] *Ibid.*, Section 64:35–36.

[4] Whitney, *Life of Heber C. Kimball*, pp. 196–97.   [5] *Ibid.*, p. 198.

real sense. Nor did he imagine himself in their position as Adam Smith would say. The individual immediately and directly felt the sufferings of his brother. And he did it because he found himself within the life of his brother. Regarded from the point of view of group consciousness, Bulter is quite right when he says "that we were made for society" and "that the principle of benevolence is as natural in man as is self-love."

The mistake which Adam Smith made (and which was also made by the moral sense school) is in treating the individual's life as distinct from that of his brother. The brother is regarded too much as the *other* person. Fellow-feeling is impossible toward individuals considered as *others*. No power of imagination could have created a sympathetic feeling between the Mormons and Gentiles. This was because the behavior of the two groups toward each other had placed them in entirely different spheres. Sympathy is had only among individuals who live the same life, follow common interests, experience common joys and sorrows.

But Adam Smith recognizes the dependence of sentiments upon social relations. He says:

> Were it possible that a human creature could grow up to manhood in some solitary place, without any communication with his own species, he could no more think of his own character, of the propriety or demerit of his own sentiments and conduct, of the beauty or deformity of his own mind, than of the beauty or deformity of his own face. All these are objects which he cannot easily see, ... and with regard to which he is provided with no mirror which can present them to his view. Bring him into society, and he is immediately provided with the mirror which he wanted before. It is placed in the countenance and behavior of those he lives with, which always mark when they enter into, and when they disapprove of his sentiments; and it is here that he first sees the propriety of his own passions, and the impropriety, the beauty and deformity of his own mind.[1]

But Adam Smith did not carry his point far enough. Society is the mirror through which we see ourselves but it is more than that: it is in society that we actually find ourselves. We actually grow up in the mirror, and are nothing apart from it. All human sentiments originate in society, and by it are maintained and given direction.

The sympathetic feelings are highly relative. They depend upon social affiliation. An individual may have a kindly feeling toward the members of his own group and the greatest animosity toward the members of another group. In fact the moral sentiments are largely dependent upon group consciousness. Altruism, charity, benevolence, pity,

---

[1] Rand, *The Classical Moralists*, p. 456.

and all forms of fellow-feeling are, according to our observation of Mormon group life, essentially a matter of group consciousness.

The conclusions of our investigation of the early period in Mormon history may thus be briefly summarized. In the first place we have observed that the moral sentiments of the Mormons have developed out of group life. These sentiments were reflected through the God of the group, who took sides with the oppressed against the oppressors. Sympathy toward the members of the group and animosity toward the members of the other group grew side by side, tending to show that these sentiments mutually support each other. The morality of this period we thus found to be essentially on the level of group morality. The individual's life was almost completely immersed in that of his group. The great virtue was loyalty and the great sin apostasy. The moral self, being so completely identified with the group, is impulsive, imitative, and sentimental.

II

The ethics of the second period is made up of the group sentiments of the first period and the new moral values which grew out of the colonizing problem of the second period. The moral standards are now tending to become more materialistic and more practical. The sermons are not now so much concerned with the war between God and the devil, between Israel and Babylon as they are with such subjects as obedience to authority, the strength of union, the sacredness of marriage, and the glory of a large posterity, the blessings of industry and the curse of idleness. The good man is now not only loyal to the group but efficient in its service.

The closing days of the life of Heber C. Kimball were spent in pioneering the new country. His activities were typical of the Mormon leaders at that time. It is interesting to compare his life in Utah with that of Joseph Smith and other Mormon leaders of the first period. In reference to his activity Apostle Whitney writes:

Preaching, colonizing, traveling through the settlements, encouraging the Saints in their toils and sacrifices, sitting in council among the leaders in Israel, ministering in sacred and holy places, and otherwise laboring for and blessing the Lord's people—so wore away the remaining years of President Kimball. . . . . His name was literally a "household word" in Israel. "Brother Heber" was everywhere honored and beloved.[1]

Thus, in the first period the Mormon prophets led the "hosts of Israel" against Babylon; they were at constant war with the enemies of God and his people. In the second period the prophets of "Israel" were laboring

[1] *Life of Heber C. Kimball*, p. 441.

for and blessing the Saints and sitting in council among their brethren. The new problems had created new demands, another class of virtue, a new type of prophet.

The new social and economic demands required something more than implicit faith in the divinity of Joseph Smith's mission and more than mere loyalty to the group; it required foresight, direction, rational leadership, system, and organization. The leaders of the people must now prove their right to lead by their ability to serve their brethren. The institutions of Mormonism must prove their divinity by their capacity to function. Thus, utility and efficiency were added to the group sentiments already established. The social self is not now merely the Mormon group fighting the gentile group; it is the self engaged in building up a great kingdom and one that is fully conscious of its detailed demands such as the constructing of roads, canals, forts, planting colonies, raising large families and going on missions. The moral individual is one who is willing to join in these many enterprises, who is industrious, unselfish, and possesses the ability to serve the community in realizing its aims.

The moral ideals and principles of social control, we shall see, were influenced by the problem then confronting the group. The great problem was to establish Zion in the mountains, to build up the Kingdom of God. And this, as we have observed in Part II, was more than a mere spiritual ideal, it was a very real task which the new condition had imposed upon the people. To realize it, meant life to the community and to fail, meant death and destruction. There were three ways in which the individual might serve his community in realizing this end: (1) as a colonizer, i.e., one who was efficient in any sort of economic community enterprise; (2) as a missionary to carry on the great proselyting program so essential in developing a strong population; and (3) as a patriarch, the head of a large family.

1. The colonization program embraced every line of economic activity and consequently every man, woman, and child capable of doing any kind of labor was actively engaged in this enterprise. The whole undertaking being essentially a community affair was conducted under the supervision of the priesthood. Thus, besides being industrious and socially efficient, the individual must obey the authority of the priesthood. This relationship is clearly revealed in an extract from a letter written by President Heber C. Kimball, to his son then on a mission to England. The letter was dated February, 1856.

There has been court in session here for weeks and weeks and I suppose that one hundred and fifty or two hundred of the brethren have been hanging around, with the council house filled to the brim. This scenery continuing for a long time, one day Brother Brigham sent Thomas Bullock to take their names, for the purpose of giving them missions, if they had not anything to do of any more importance. So Brother Brigham counseled me to make a selection— for Los Vegas, some thirty, who are ordered to sell their possessions and go with their families as soon as the weather will permit, for the purpose of going down on to the Rio Virgin to raise cotton; another company of forty-eight to go to Green River to strengthen up that settlement, make farms, build mills, etc., and some thirty-five or forty to go north to Salmon River, ... some thirty to go to Carson Valley, ... some thirty to go into the lead business near the Los Vegas; and eight to go to the East Indies. There are eighteen called to Europe, and seven to Australia.[1]

This right which the ecclesiastical authorities held over those of lower rank in all matters of community concern is very significant. Although a strong group spirit had been created long before this and although people had been disciplined in obedience to group authority before they undertook colonization in the mountain valleys, yet the unity of action prior to this time was that of direct group control. A strong group spirit was felt by every individual. The constant pressure from an opposing group made the members within the Mormon group very sensitive to social suggestions. But this warm, first-hand spiritual control was not possible in the new situation where the external social pressure had been practically removed and where the communities were scattered among the valleys of the great mountainous country. The control must now become more a matter of personal authority.

But although the control now became centered in individuals who held the priesthood there was still a recognition of the group back of this priestly authority. The priesthood is the authority of God and symbolizes the authority and power of the group. By means of this symbol and the recognition which it received, the colonizing enterprises could be systematically carried on. But for the leader in this period priesthood alone was not sufficient; the situation, without minimizing the importance of the former, demanded ability also. And in this respect the demand is greater than that of both the first and third periods. The economic situation was too grave for a man who was not efficient and useful to the people to remain long at the head of a colony. The people were now conscious of the purpose of leadership, and the successful pioneer could command obedience because he actually became a hero in the great struggle.

[1] *Life of Heber C. Kimball*, pp. 420–21.

But not only did the colonizing problem create a new relation between the people and the priesthood, it created a new attitude within the group, of the individuals toward one another.   The brotherly feeling was now developed on a utilitarian basis.   The brother was needed in the building of canals, roads, and forts.   The manufacturing and commercial activities demanded united effort.   On every hand the individual found himself compelled to co-operate with his brethren.   This co-operative effort was felt to be so important that many of the colonizing enterprises were preceded by a rebaptism for the purpose of bringing "the new colony under perfect organization, socially as well as ecclesiastically."[1]   Out of this practical co-operative relationship, this common struggle to build up their Zion, we have a moral relation of a higher order than that which maintained in early Mormon history.   The moral sentiments developed out of a more practical and more normal social relation.   The self enlarged to include others in a more complex system of values.   John Stuart Mill's explanation of moral sympathy is quite adequate here:

Not only does strengthening of social ties, and all healthy growth of society, give to each individual a stronger personal interest in practically consulting the welfare of others, it also leads him to identify his feelings more and more with their good. . . . . He comes, as though instinctively, to be conscious of himself as a being who of course pays regard to others.   The good of others becomes to him a thing naturally and necessarily to be attended to, like any of the physical conditions of our existence.[2]

2. Just as every good man in Israel was an active colonizer at that time, so every man was expected to fulfil a foreign mission.   In fact proselyting was a part of the colonizing scheme.   The following taken from the official organ of the church (1851) illustrates how the colonizing and the proselyting work of the church went hand in hand.

The estimated fifteen thousand inhabitants in Deseret, the past year, have raised grain sufficient to sustain the thirty thousand for the coming year, inspire us confidently to believe that the thirty thousand the coming year can raise sufficient for sixty thousand the succeeding year and to this great object and end our energies will be exerted to double our population annually. . . . . [3]

Thus we may note, besides the hopeful spirit which is here revealed concerning the growth of Zion, the unity of purpose which underlies both the colonizing and the missionary work.   It was regarded as a matter of course that the Saints at home should prepare to feed and care for the thousands who were to immigrate every year.   Brigham Young said:

[1] *Tullidge's Magazine*, III (July, 1884), 233.

[2] Quoted by Rand, *The Classical Moralists*, pp. 666–67.

[3] *Millennial Star*, XIII (1851), 51.

It is also a true principle that a man should keep not only his property but himself upon the altar, ready for sacrifice at any moment; to do with all his might the will of his maker regardless of the consequences to his property or himself or any thing that pertains to him.[1]

But not only were the missionaries expected to increase the Mormon population but they were to furnish the community with skilled mechanics. In a later volume of the same paper we read the following instructions from the mission president to the conference presidents:

The first presidency of the church at the Valley has sent express instruction in relation to all kinds of mechanics and manufacturers. . . . . And now is the time that they are wanted, for they are situated at a vast distance from all civilized nations of the earth. . . . . In order that we may become great and flourish as a people, it is highly necessary that we have manufacturers in our own midst. . . . .[2]

Thus in regard to this stage of Mormon ethics Hume is right when he says: "The social virtues are never regarded without their beneficial tendencies, nor viewed as barren and unfruitful" and that "utility . . . . forms, at least, a part of their merit, and is one source of that approbation and regard so universally paid to them."[3] The sentiments created by the group struggle of the first period were not weakened by the conception of utility which the second period in Mormon history tended to develop. The brotherly feeling now received meaning. It was now consciously desired. It becomes a real standard which the individual endeavors to attain himself and which he requires of his associates.

3. The control of sex relationship has always constituted one of the most important moral problems of the race. Social customs have always served as the strongest factor in this as in every other vital social moral relation. Monogamy has, through ages of social evolution, come to be the form of sex relation generally adhered to among different peoples. While individuals among civilized as well as among primitive peoples, at times, violate the social customs it is very extraordinary for an entire people to depart arbitrarily from the established form of marriage relations. Especially is it surprising for a church to assume the responsibility in the Christian era when sex purity and celibacy were regarded as among the greatest virtues. Our problem here is to explain how the Mormon mind could be brought to justify morally the institution of polygamy or the patriarchal form of marriage.

[1] Brigham Young, *ibid.*, XIV, 214.

[2] *Ibid.*, XVI, 362.

[3] Quoted by Rand, *The Classical Moralists*, p. 431.

If moral values existed apart from the life of the social group or if they were the outcome of pure reflective processes it would be a difficult task indeed to account for this radical departure from general social sanction. But when we apply our principle that moral values are really group sentiments and that they depend on the one hand upon group tradition and on the other hand upon the immediate vital problems of the group the explanation is not difficult.

The Mormons, we have seen, had identified themselves with ancient Israel. The sentiments and traditions of that ancient people became the sentiments and traditions of Mormonism. On the other hand, the Mormons had almost completely isolated themselves both socially and physically from all civilized peoples. They lived in a different atmosphere from that of the peoples of the world. The sentiments of "Babylon" were not to control their lives. They hated Babylon and any departure from its ways was regarded by them as righteousness. But they loved Israel and longed to imitate its institutions. Thus they considered polygamy, which was of Israel, more sacred than monogamy which was the common practice of the rebellious world.

But polygamy was also justified on the basis of utility. The patriarchal order tended to increase the Mormon population and thus added strength to the kingdom. Brigham Young, Heber C. Kimball, Orson Pratt, Lorin Farr, and scores of other patriarchs[1] who had no fewer than forty and some even more than sixty children were the great men of Israel. Should this system have continued and should the members of the church have followed generally the example of their leaders, Zion would soon have felt its strength through its growing population. This was no doubt the motive which led President Woodruff to remark that the "church and Kingdom could not advance without it" and that "the leading men of Israel who are presiding over stakes will have to obey the law of Abraham" or resign.[2]

The moral self thus became identified with the new and more complex aims of the group. Sentiments grew up about these interests until they became sacred and, as we shall see in our next division, fixed attitudes of mind. Thus, to the old group sentiments of the first period which formed the subconscious basis of the Mormon ethical life, we have added utilitarian ideals and standards, all of which are transmitted to the third period.

[1] Whitney, *History of Utah*, Vol. IV.

[2] Cowley's *Life of Wilford Woodruff*, p. 542.

III

The transition from the second to the third stage of Mormonism is marked by two important conditions, the coming to a close of the great colonization movement and the abandonment of the patriarchal order of marriage. In consequence of this, the Kingdom of God was deprived of its real, concrete, and material content and began to be defined more in terms of a church organization and spiritual authority. The New Jerusalem was still the social ideal but no longer a city to be built immediately in this world but one which Christ will build when he returns to earth. The material aims tended to become spiritual ideals.

Heretofore very slight distinction was made between the spiritual and the temporal affairs of the church. They all belonged to the Kingdom of God and the church claimed the right to exercise its authority in any direction. But when sufficient private capital had accumulated and the individuals began to feel their own strength and could undertake business enterprises without the aid of the church, its influence in economic matters began to decline. The state began to assume greater responsibility and was becoming stronger in all lines of general community interest. The individuals were beginning to assert themselves through the institutions of the state. The church was forced to confine its activities to that sphere in which the older group sentiments still hold sway. Its sphere was becoming less temporal and more spiritual. Its attention was being turned to its traditions, and its function was becoming more and more that of conserving its institutions and group sentiments.

This new situation has put the church on the defensive. Its problem now is to protect its own sentiments and institutions and to defend the faith. The good man now is a staunch defender of the institutions and true to the faith. The following hymn reveals the sentiments which the orthodox members are struggling to establish among the youth:

> Shall the youth of Zion falter,
>   In defending truth and right?
> While the enemy assaileth,
>   Shall we shrink, or shun the fight? No!

> True to the faith that our parents have cherished;
>   True to the truth for which martyrs have perished;
> To God's command, soul, heart, and hand,
>   Faithful and true we will ever stand.[1]

[1] *Songs of Zion*, No. 179.

Just as the foregoing hymn illustrates the stress that is placed on old sentiments so the following statement from a recent sermon illustrates the attention that is now given to laws, form, and institutions.

God has given unto his children a code of laws: faith, repentance, and baptism by immersion for the remission of sins, by those who have authority, to administer in the ordinances of his kingdom, the laying on of hands for the gift of the Holy Ghost, the law of tithing, the law of consecration, the law of sealing ordinances in the house wherein man and woman are sealed for time and all eternity, and all the various cardinal principles of the gospel. These are the laws of our being, unto which we must subscribe if we would inherit the earth when it has lived its laws, that we may live upon it many, many years.[1]

Of these "cardinal principles" faith is the most basic. It is the sacred duty of every member of the church to believe implicitly in the divinity of Jesus Christ, in the revelations of Joseph Smith, in the authenticity of the Book of Mormon, in miracles and spiritual gifts. He must believe in the divinity of the priesthood and in the idea that all the organizations of the church are sacred institutions established by God. He must accept the literal interpretation of the Bible. The man who does not have this state of mind is not a good man in a positive sense. Morality without faith is negative and does not lead to the highest spiritual life. Faith means spirituality "and without spirituality there can be no vital living morality."

The following brief statements made by church authorities in the recent general conferences illustrate the importance that is now attached to faith. According to C. W. Nibley the mission of Mormonism is to protect the faith.

Now here is the mission of Mormonism. Here is the great need of this church, that faith shall not be abolished from the earth, from the hearts of the children of men. . . . . We believe in education, but some of us send our children away from home to be educated, and many of them come back seemingly determined to claim relationship with the apes rather than with angels.[2]

According to Reed Smoot, Christianity is endangered by heresy.

I care not for the cranks that may arise from time to time, for their lives are short; but it seems to me that when a man like Dr. Charles Eliot . . . . comes out and announces as a new doctrine a faith that denies the divinity of Jesus Christ, that denies that man is made in God's image, that denies the authenticity of all biblical miracles, the efficacy of prayer, the supernatural value of sacrament, the merit of self-sacrifice, and even denies the immortality of the soul, it strikes me . . . . that there is danger for Christianity among the people.[3]

[1] W. H. Smart, *Eighty-seventh Annual Conference Report*, pp. 95–96.

[2] *Eighty-first Annual Conference Report*, pp. 54–55.

[3] *General Conference Report for 1909.*

Faith is worth more than life according to Joseph F. Smith:

Every device possible to the understanding and ingenuity of cunning men is being used for the purpose of diverting our children from the faith of the gospel and from the love of truth. . . . . I would rather take one of my children to the grave than I would see him turn away from this gospel.[1]

This defensive attitude of the orthodox Mormons reflects the present conflict. Faith in church dogma has become a moral value which has grown out of the present social situation. It is the great virtue of today just as loyalty was the great virtue in the first period, or efficiency and industry in the second period of Mormon history.

To honor the priesthood in the pioneer days meant to obey those who were endowed with its authority. But high priestly authority and capacity for leadership usually went together. In fact the priesthood increased its power and sanctity through the social service which it rendered. It possessed utility and could command obedience because of it. To honor the priesthood in recent years is not so much a matter of obeying it for the purpose of realizing a material benefit as it is to recognize its divinity and refrain from criticizing and speaking ill against the "Lord's Anointed." This attitude toward the ecclesiastical authorities, like the attitude toward faith has grown out of internal conditions. It results from the growing critical spirit among the younger members of the church. The orthodox element feels a need for putting itself on the defense. Thus says Joseph F. Smith:

Fathers and mothers in Israel, will you try to teach your children . . . . that the Prophet Joseph Smith restored again to the earth the priesthood which was held by Peter, James, and John. Teach your children to respect their bishops and the teachers that come to their homes to teach them. . . . . teach them to honor the priesthood which you hold.[2]

As the controlling power of the group weakens, the priestly authority becomes less positive. Thus Brigham Young could command when the prophet of today may only advise and counsel. Brigham Young could exercise the authority of the priesthood in nearly every line of community or individual interests. The present leader must confine the exercise of his priestly influence within certain limits. These limits are fixed by group sentiments. When he extends his activity into political and industrial affairs he meets with opposition from those who do not feel the old group sentiments. Only the older members of the church

[1] *General Conference*, 1909, pp. 2-8.

[2] *Eighty-seventh Annual Conference Report*, p. 5.

recognize the voice of a prophet in these matters. The following remark of Apostle Talmage illustrates the situation and the struggle which the church leaders are having to maintain the desired attitude toward the prophet:

I have met here and there a disgruntled one, one who is saying,"Why don't we receive further revelation from God today?" We are receiving it day by day. . . . . If ever the church of Christ was led by a prophet enjoying communion with God . . . . and none of us can doubt such leadership in the past —this day witnesses that condition. I testify unto you that the man who stands at the head of this church is the mouth piece of God unto his people, and if we fail to heed his words, his admonitions, his instruction given unto us as they have been, and are, in love and nevertheless with firmness and with no uncertainty of tone, we bring ourselves under condemnation.[1]

Again, since the priesthood represents the authority of the group and since the power of this authority depends upon the traditional attitudes and old group sentiments, the field of its activity tends to be limited largely to the preservation of forms and sentiments already established. Thus, unlike conditions in the colonizing period when the initiative was taken by the higher church authorities, today the social reform movements in Mormon communities are undertaken by the younger men and women, who hold subordinate positions in the church.

Thus, out of active, enthusiastic, and practical group sentiments has emerged a system of formal laws or duties. What were once means to an end have now become ends in themselves. Tithing was once a means to the building up of God's kingdom but now it is a duty to pay tithing whether the church needs the money or not. It is a duty for a man to go on a mission when called by the divine authority although he may question his qualifications to preach the gospel. It is his duty to have faith in all the doctrines of Mormonism although his experience may lead him to doubt the validity of some of them.

In conclusion, let us review the evolution of Mormon ethics with reference to our three basic psychological principles. In the first place we have observed that the moral self was identical with the social or group self. In the first stage the self was completely merged in the group. The moral life was therefore relatively simple, to be loyal to "Israel" and remain responsive to the suggestions of the group. In the second period, the group developed more complex aims. The moral self became more reflective and less impulsive. The individual was now able to distinguish between his social self and his egoistic self. In the third stage the social self is identified with the traditional and customary atti-

[1] *Eighty-eighth Annual Conference Report*, p. 161.

tudes of the group. The moral self is now one who keeps the faith and observes the laws and forms of the church.

Altruism and egotism are thus found to be relative matters. In the early group conflict the Mormon people were egotistic in their relations with the opposite group but very altruistic in dealing with one another. However, not until the economic problems of the second period presented themselves did the people become fully conscious of this as a moral principle. It was the removal of the external social pressure and the concentration of attention upon the group's own welfare which made it possible for the individuals to recognize a moral obligation as such. But even in the second period moral obligation did not often extend beyond the members of the group. However, in the third stage, the growing commercial, political, and educational intercourse with the outside world is having the effect of extending sympathetic relations and a sense of obligation to people outside of the group.

As to our second proposition, we have observed that the moral evolution was essentially an evolution of sentiments. The early group life was impulsive and emotional and out of this developed the most basic and permanent Mormon sentiments. These sentiments became definitely attached to certain persons, institutions, and events. In the second period other sentiments developed, peculiar to the pioneer life. All these sentiments have accumulated and represent in the third period very definite and fixed attitudes. The orthodox Mormon has always found morality on the side of these sentiments, and associated immorality with the spirit and life which has opposed them.

But these group sentiments, as we have observed, are well personified in the God of Israel. This personification has made the transition from one stage of Mormon moral standards to another more obvious. Thus, in the first stage, God was engaged in protecting his "chosen people" and punishing the "rebellious." Under His special direction the Saints were led in battle against the devil and his followers. The true servant of God at that time was one who was loyal and submissive to the will of God. In the second period, God became the deliverer of Israel from the persecution of the enemy. He led his people to a land of refuge. He made their land productive and increased their storehouses. He assigned his people a practical task, to build up his kingdom. An efficient servant was rewarded with a home in Zion, with a large family and with flocks and herds. In the third period, God has become a law giver to his people and a defender of his priesthood and the sacred institutions of the group. The reward for righteousness is now spiritual; it is salvation in the Kingdom of Heaven.

CHAPTER XII

THE POSSIBILITIES FOR ADJUSTMENT

From the practical point of view the outcome of the present internal conflict is a most vital question. The maladjustment which existed between the Mormons and the Gentiles is practically overcome, and so is that between the Mormons and the arid country. We have observed the strife between science and Mormon theology, the contradiction between the business interest of the priesthood and the spirit of industrial democracy, we have observed the contentions occasioned by the Mormon marriage institutions and finally traced the development of Mormon ethical ideals and standards. In treating these problems we have been concerned more with the interpretation of the different factors involved in the conflict than with the social value of the process itself. What will these tendencies lead to, and of what practical value are they to the group? These are questions deserving attention.

The dogmatic opponent of Mormonism regards all of its institutions as positively bad and as directly hindering progress. To him the solution of the problem is the elimination of all that is Mormon. The orthodox Mormon, on the other hand, believes that all the institutions of his church are divine and essential to the great plan of human salvation. His solution of the problem is the silencing of critics and heretics. The ideal situation, in his mind, is for every member of the church to accept with implicit faith every word that falls from the lips of the prophet and obey unhesitatingly the authority of the priesthood. Or as one of the apostles of the church expressed it: "I would that the faith of all Israel increased to the point that every man, woman, and child would say, 'I know not save the Lord commandeth.'" To the unprejudiced mind neither of these attitudes points the way to progress.

Conflict is neither bad nor good in itself. It may result in destruction or it may be the condition for progressive reconstruction. The internal conflict simply reveals the fact that a crisis has come and a change is about to take place. This change may destroy the group life or it may strengthen it. The crisis is a warning of approaching danger and an opportunity for progress. Without it Mormon religious life would be reduced to a dead level. Such is the case in some of the rural communities where the new critical spirit has not yet expressed itself. In such places religious discussion consists largely of repeating religious dogma, retelling the old Mormon and gentile struggles and relating the experiences of the pioneers. Even in some of the general conferences of the church in Salt Lake City, the sameness of thought and expression becomes so monotonous that the most sympathetic member indicates weariness. But the majority of the people favor harmony rather than discord for the former is the true spirit of the gospel, but confusion is prompted by the devil.

The proper adjustment is not to be brought about by prohibiting criticism nor can it be made by eliminating wholly the old institutions and traditions. Criticism provides the occasion for readjustment and progress. On the other hand institutions and traditions tend to retain the social standards already established and give stability to the life of the community. They function in the life of the community just as habits do in the individual. They form the automatic side of conduct, maintain unity and order among the basic relations of life, and thus set free the voluntary elements of consciousness to work out new modes of behavior. They constitute fundamental factors in the control of the individual life as well as in that of the social group. Progress may build more certain attainments by utilizing these historical accumulations than by ignoring them. The reason why many social revolutions have failed to realize very valuable aims is because the basic factors of social control were disregarded. No effective reconstruction in Mormonism will be had unless its sentiments and institutions are turned to good account. Real progress presupposes proper social continuity.

To overcome the present maladjustment two concessions must be made. On the one hand every institution of Mormonism must be subjected to the searchlight of science, and scientific truths, in so far as they provide human welfare, must be considered as sacred as religious truths. On the other hand the educators of Utah must be willing to analyze the Mormon institutions with the true impartial attitude and recognize the desirable as well as the undesirable qualities. In short, prejudice must be removed from both sides before real progress can be attained. The ideal situation will be more fully realized when the church will make more frequent use of scientific experts to aid in its many educational enterprises, and when the college graduate will regard the church, of which he is a member, as an organization through which he can render social and moral service.

We have already discussed in different connections the importance of attention in determining the various aspects of the spiritual life of

Mormonism. We have observed how the strong concentration of group attention added divinity to the leaders, magnified the importance of historical events and places and how, through this factor, institutions became sacred. A long history of such centralized group consciousness accompanied by great emotional excitement has created strong Mormon sentiments toward the past and its accumulations of institutions so that it is difficult to direct attention upon present-day problems. Many of the Mormons seem to live by themselves in a world constructed out of their past group life, a distinct world of discourse.

In addition to this group sentiment which directs attention toward the past there is a sort of Mormon scholasticism which has, in recent years, engaged the attention of some of the educated members of the church. It has one purpose—that of justifying the Mormon dogmas. This peculiar rationalizing tendency has developed side by side with heresy which it is constantly endeavoring to silence by argument. Besides a large number of books written with this aim, the church theological classes are making use of this line of reasoning. The old institutions and traditions are thus fortified on the one hand by sentiment and on the other by a well-developed system of theology.

Opposed to these conservative Mormon theologians stand those who are effectively bringing about a readjustment in both thought and sentiment. These people do not present direct opposition. They tend to shift the attention to the more vital problems of the day. They emphasize the present rather than the past, the immediate rather than the remote, the concrete rather than the abstract.

Among the most important of the conditions that tend to bring about readjustment is the rapid growth of colleges and high schools in the state as well as a tendency for a large number of young people to seek education outside of the state. Between four and five thousand young people of Mormon parentage are attending college every year and many times that number are in high schools. They are thus coming in contact with the educational spirit and developing a great many new ideals and values. The many possibilities of the larger life, social and scientific, are being forced upon them. These new interests are not regarded as antagonistic to the Mormon ideals, but little by little they detract the attention from creed and abstract theology.

The lines of educational interest which most directly influence this reconstruction are those of the social sciences. Courses in sociology, economics, political science, ethics of citizenship, social psychology, the psychology of religion and the scientific study of the Bible are all related directly to the local problem. Unlike some other scientific courses these not only raise the problems of interest and detract attention from the non-essentials, but they raise the main questions of conflict and point the way of adjustment. Thus young people are beginning to view the church in an objective manner and judge its institutions upon their merits. This free discussion of institutions is an "admission" that questions of authority and of dogma are not absolutely settled. When a sacred subject is once admitted to discussion it tends to lose its divinity and sometimes its vitality as a factor in control.

But while it is important that the institutions of a social group should be subject to criticism, this examination and introspection may, like the institutions, become an end itself. Institutions are not made by the power of reason altogether nor are they reformed for practical use by such a conscious effort. They are made and reshaped to a large extent while the group is in action. The more or less blind forward movement plays also its part in selection, creation, and readaptation of both the conscious life and the social institutions. Analysis and criticism inhibits natural expression of impulses in the group as well as in the individual. It creates friction and results in the loss of energy. The Mormon group was most active when it centered its attention upon some thing outside of itself, upon an opposing group or upon some obstacle of its environment. Then thought looked outward rather than inward, and seemed to possess wonderful vitality. The group built cities, as it were, in a day; it endured great privation; it met and surmounted a variety of obstacles. But it is with a social group as with an individual, it tends to lose its vigor as soon as it becomes self-conscious. Its spirit weakens as soon as it begins to think about itself.

If the youth of Mormonism remain content with the mere rationalization and criticism of their inherited institutions, nothing worth while will be accomplished; they will end where they began, in mere reflection. What Mormonism needs today is the vitalization of its institutions, which need to be put into use rather than merely contemplated. They should function as means rather than be analyzed as ends. When Mormonism finds more glory in working out new social ideals than in the contemplating of past achievements or the beauty of its own theological system, it will begin to feel its old-time strength. The group spirit will reappear in a new form.

Mormonism of today needs to emphasize its social problems, those which are felt to be vital by all its classes, its sentimentalists, its rationalists, its critics. It needs to emphasize problems which will engage the attention of all of these; one which will unify the varied interests and at the same time force the attention away from itself. They must be problems to which every member of the church will respond. They should stimulate feeling and thought, and above all, they must stimulate action.

There is a demand for a leadership which not only possesses the sentiments of the group but which is responsive to the social and moral impulses of the times. The men who feel the spirit and needs of the hour, who are in direct contact with all the new relations of life, may be able to unite the contending factions and become the leaders of the present and future generations of Mormonism.

INDEX

Abraham, received concubines, 16, 75
Abram, Lord said to, 15, 16
Ames, E. S., quoted, 35, 73

Bishop, the temporal officer, 5
Brigham Young University, instruction and conflict, 64, 65
Brimhall, G. H., quoted, 66

Caldwell County, 22
Clay County, 21
Colonization: three problems of, 40; methods of, 42, 43, 44, 45; proselyting as a means of, 43, 44
Communistic ideal, origin of, 17
Conflict: causes of, 29, 30; significance of, 97
Co-operation: commercial, 52, 53, 54, 55; in manufacturing, 50, 51, 52
Criticism: institutions subject to, 99; spirit of, 61, 62, 63, 64, 65

Doctrine and Covenants, defined, 6

Faith, as an ideal, 92
Families, large, 46, 90

God, as Spirit of group, 24, 95
Godbeite Movement, 60, 61
Group consciousness, 19, 20, 21, 22, 23, 24; stages in development of, 59

Hume, theory of, 89

Immigration, 43, 44, 45, 46
Institutions: business, 69, 70; as products of past experience, 67
Irrigation: co-operative origin of, 41, 42; necessity of, 40, 41; practices in Egypt and by Indian tribes, 40

Jackson County, sacred land, 18, 24
James, William, quoted, 13

Marriage: patriarchal order of, 16; spiritual covenant of, 73
Migration, organization for, 37, 38, 39
Mill, John Stuart, ethical theory of, 88
Missouri, expulsion from, 21, 22, 23
Morality, group, 82, 83

Mormonism: and Christianity, 17; embraces temporal interests, 4; as a process of adjustment, 9; origin of, 14; moral stages in, 80

Nauvoo, an independent city, 26
Nibley, C. W., quoted, 92

Penrose, C. W., quoted, 64
Persecution, cause of, 19
Polygamy: as cause of conflict, 76; origin of, 75
President, power of, 6
Priesthood, authority and responsibility of, 5, 94
Psychology, functional, 3

Revenue system, 6, 7
Rigdon, Sidney, associated with Joseph Smith, 17; quoted, 23

Scholasticism in Mormonism, 98
Secret Constitution, 19
Smith, Adam, theory of, 84
Smith, Joseph: character of, 27, 28; inspired by group, 27, 28; sentiment of group toward, 29; religious genius, 14; use of Bible language and Israelitish ideals, 15
Smith, Joseph F., quoted, 4, 5, 67, 71, 72
Smoot, Reed, quoted, 92

Taylor, John, quoted, 54
Thomas, W. I., quoted, 74
Tithing, 6, 66, 67, 68, 92
Tullidge, E. W., quoted, 51

Union Pacific Railroad, commercial significance of, 49, 52
United Order: argument for, 51; nature of, 5

Veblin, quoted, 66

Woodruff, Wilford, quoted, 76, 78

Young, Brigham: inspired by group, 47; leadership, 36; quoted, 45

Zion's Co-operative Mercantile Institution, 53, 54, 55
Zion, Land of, 15, 18